PACKED AND READY

For decades one of the "lovely wives" obscured by position,
identity melded into his, only he and she knowing
her invisible name tag wrought by what hears birds on the morning
or lifts prayers into dreams into unselfconscious becoming:

    the handling of children's awakenings like hot bread
    from the oven of knowing how for fevers or bruises,
    the keen apprehension of too much or too little,
    the quieting of fears with affectionate laughter,

    the pouring in of humor to lighten a pot of message,
    the girl still dancing in too-long-stood-on legs,
    behind the bright eyes the bright head the bright soul
    a metaphor for leavening hearts like yeast in dough.

Irresistible the tuning, the measure of health
like green finding its way on a grey day in early spring
or a bag packed for untimed leaving
on command of love needing a hand and

closeness closer than staying behind in body or spirit,
the gracious accompaniment among strangers
reaching and being reached, those lucky or unlucky before
made to know "special" in a moment of resurrection:

    brief as a talk at a pulpit
    lasting not as a leap, but a succession
    of brief, amazing risings,
    each one making possible the next

    for whoever is present in the radiant presence
    of this woman, this lovely wife, this forever young woman
    replete in knowing exactly how,
    abundant in aging, personification of radiant faith.

She is a vivid body of good, graced by
a loving God's expectation and surely fulfillment
packed shining and ready for whatever
and when.

                    —*Emma Lou Thayne*

Glimpses into the Life and Heart of Marjorie Pay Hinckley

Virginia H. Pearce, EDITOR

DESERET BOOK COMPANY
SALT LAKE CITY, UTAH

Photo credits:
Page 46, photo by Stuart Johnson/*Deseret News*
Page 90, photo by Kristan Jacobsen/*Church News*
Page 109, photo by Stuart Johnson/*Church News*
Pages 152 and 173, photos by Richard M. Romney. © 1998 by Intellectual Reserve, Inc. Used by permission
Page 157, photo by Craig Dimond. © 1998 by Intellectual Reserve, Inc. Used by permission
Page 183, photo by Don Busath
Page 191, photo by Leah Hogsten/*Salt Lake Tribune*

Library of Congress Cataloging-in-Publication Data

Glimpses into the life and heart of Marjorie Pay Hinckley / edited by
  Virginia H. Pearce.
    p.   cm.
  Includes index.
  ISBN 1-57345-523-7
  1. Hinckley, Marjorie Pay. 2. Mormon women—Religious life.
I. Hinckley, Marjorie Pay. II. Pearce, Virginia H.
BX8695.H57G57   1999
289.3'092—dc21
  [B]   99-10317
                                                                CIP

Printed in the United States of America   18961-0278R
R. R. Donnelley and Sons, Crawfordsville, IN

10   9

For
Georgetta Paxman Pay
and daffodils

CONTENTS

viii

FOREWORD

*

BY SHERI DEW

I will never forget the afternoon I had Marjorie Hinckley all to myself. The setting was her comfortable condominium home in Salt Lake City, and my excuse for imposing on her time was a formal interview about her life with her husband, President Gordon B. Hinckley. I quickly found, however, that Marjorie Hinckley is not formal—gracious, yes; dignified, delightful, unassuming, absolutely. But formal? That's a word I would never use to describe Sister Hinckley, who has an uncanny knack for making anyone her friend and bolstering the person's spirits in the process. I call it Marjorie's Magic, the spell this diminutive woman casts that sends you away feeling light-years better about yourself than you did when you entered her presence. It is a sensation that combines total acceptance and *joie de vivre*, an optimism and enthusiasm about life that, if transmitted to society at large, would put therapists and pundits permanently out of business.

That afternoon in her condo I might have wished for the clock to stand still. It was pure delight to listen in as she reminisced about the unexpected and even dramatic twists and turns her life has taken during her sixty-plus years as the wife of President Gordon B. Hinckley.

She recalled their teenage years together in Salt Lake City's Liberty Stake, where Gordon's father served as stake president for more than a decade. They had attended different high schools—he went to LDS High School, and she to East High— but in the after-school hours they had found themselves in the same crowd. She had been impressed from the outset with the skinny young man who shared her sense of humor but also demonstrated a more serious, studious side. Their first date was to a Gold and Green Ball when she was eighteen. That night she told her mother, "This young man is going somewhere."

Their relationship continued to blossom, and they dated fairly steadily for some time. Even still, when Gordon left in 1933 to serve in the European Mission headquartered in London, he and Marjorie had not made any promises to each other. But each quietly hoped that the other would still be interested two and a half years hence.

As it turned out, they were. And their courtship picked up where it had left off. Though it didn't take long for either of them to realize that they were meant for each other, they didn't marry immediately. It was, after all, the *bottom of the Depression*, as he would refer to it ever after, and marriage in that nerve-wracking economic climate was something people didn't jump into without serious planning and a generous dose of caution and courage.

As Sister Hinckley relived for me the events leading up to

their April 1937 marriage, she said something I will never forget. "When Gordon came home from his mission," she remembered, "I could tell that he had changed. I had always known he was remarkable, but now there was something even more distinctive about him. As we dated and then became engaged to be married, something became obvious to me. I knew that he loved me, and that he would always be good to me. But I also knew that I would never come first with him." She paused for a moment before adding, "And that was okay."

When I suggested that some women might balk at such a situation, she replied: "I knew Gordon was going to devote his life to the Lord. And I couldn't think of anyone I'd rather have him devoted to."

Her statement was so matter-of-fact that she might as well have been rattling off the grocery list. There was no self-pity or evidence of any grand sacrifice on her part, nor was there any sense of self-congratulation, just an expression of her simple faith and mature spiritual equilibrium. At that moment, it was clear to me that she had been perfectly suited to stand at the side of a man who was destined to play a vital role in the twentieth-century Church.

All of my subsequent interactions with Sister Hinckley, and particularly with the two of them together, have borne that out. It is now simply impossible for me to imagine one without the other. Not every woman would have put up with the incessant hammering, sawing, and painting that went on for months, even years, at a time as her husband turned bedrooms into kitchens and front entryways into dining rooms. Little did she know that she had married a *builder* in every sense of the word, one who would frequently remodel their home even as he labored tirelessly to build the Church and help the gospel kingdom move forward—first as an employee and later as an ordained leader.

But she has been the perfect companion for someone who is constantly forging into unknown territory, always carrying a heavy load, and never inclined to stand still. Perhaps we will never know the extent to which her wonderful sense of balance and humor have helped her husband maintain his.

Their interactions with each other demonstrate the comfortable camaraderie of their life together. During a meeting with missionaries in London's Hyde Park chapel, President Hinckley began his remarks: "I am going to exercise my prerogative and call on Sister Hinckley to talk with you. This is something for which I will pay a dear price, but so be it." He chuckled to himself as he turned from the podium. But without missing a beat, she stepped to the pulpit, lowered the microphone—she *always* has to lower the microphone—and said, "I like this man a lot, but I like him some times a lot more than others. What would you do if you were married to a man like this?" The missionaries roared their approval.

On another occasion, this time with missionaries in St. Louis, Missouri, President Hinckley began his remarks, "Sister Hinckley and I have been all over the world speaking to missionaries, and I don't know anyone who does a better job at this than she does. So I think I'd like for her to speak for a few minutes." Again, Sister Hinckley's spontaneous response invited laughter: "I'll tell you exactly why I'm speaking. President Hinckley hasn't decided yet what he wants to say, and he's stalling for time."

After warming up the group and making all in attendance feel as though they were back home with an old and trusted friend, Sister Hinckley left the missionaries with a message of hope and encouragement that set the stage perfectly for her prophet-husband. "It always gives me a lift to meet with the missionaries," she told them, "because my testimony is reborn. I can't tell you how much it means to us that you would come to spend this time with us. You strengthen our testimonies just by being here. There is no more important work in all the world, and you will never do anything more important in all your life than you are doing right now." President Hinckley then took the stand and delivered a rousing message to those missionary troops.

In every conceivable way, Sister Hinckley has stood at her husband's side. One can only imagine the number of times that her gentle encouragement, her gift for looking at life's bright side, and her unfeigned optimism have spurred him on and buoyed him up. One evening during a hectic ten-day trip to England, President Hinckley's first trip abroad after becoming President of the Church, he and Sister Hinckley were enjoying a quiet meal prior to a fireside in a Liverpool stake center. As they were sampling the British fare that President Hinckley had come to love as a young missionary, he said quietly to his wife, almost in passing and as though no one else were present, "I just don't know about this fireside tonight. I have no idea what I am supposed to say." Without so much as looking up from the table, Sister Hinckley reached over, patted her husband's knee, and said, "It will come to you. You'll know exactly what you should say." That was it. There was nothing showy or even remarkable about the interchange. But one could imagine how frequently she had demonstrated this kind of quiet support during his four decades of service as a General Authority.

Did Marjorie Hinckley ever imagine where her life would take her? "Absolutely not," she insists. "I've been busy just getting through today. But sometimes I have to pinch myself when I realize all that I've been able to see and experience. It *never* gets old. Every day is *so* exciting. When you see what's happening in this Church all over the world, you're just thrilled to wake up every morning! Life is more than I ever imagined it would be."

I believe that, just as President Gordon B. Hinckley was foreordained to serve as President of the Church, his wife was prepared to walk through life with him. Surely it would have been difficult, perhaps even impossible, for him to do all he has done had it not been for the influence of this woman whose belief in her husband has known no bounds.

She is a gift to all who fall under her magical spell. But most of all, she has proven a companion *par excellence*, a pillar of strength and stability, to a man who will ever be regarded as one of the Church's great builders.

PREFACE

*

With every published book there are questions that beg for answers: "What is this book?" and "Why was it published?" There were "working answers" for this book that began before a word was put onto paper, and additional answers that appeared with each draft and revision. So what are the answers that sift themselves to the surface as layout decisions are being finalized, cover designs considered, and those permanent machines called printing presses scheduled?

The what-is-this-book? answer begins by saying what this book is *not*. This book is not a chronological biography of events and accomplishments. Rather, its pages contain glimpses—incomplete snapshots of remembered conversations and illuminations. These glimpses are recorded by family, friends, and acquaintances. They include many of the words of the subject herself (these appear in lavender throughout the book). An appendix contains a few of the many talks she has delivered. Some entries are simply one sentence, while others are much longer attempts to explain, show, and share. Some are obvious—even clichéd. Some are more subtle. But all of the words, collectively and separately, are incomplete attempts to help others be more fully acquainted with a remarkable woman.

Remarkable in what way? Certainly not in the ways of the world. Our world hungers and thirsts after the spectacular, the exceptional. We aspire, we coerce, we compete, we gather in the trophies. And then we look for ways to escape the stress. President Spencer W. Kimball said: "We are not asking for something spectacular but rather for our sisters to find real self-fulfillment through wise self-development in the pursuit of righteous and worthy endeavors." (*My Beloved Sisters* [Salt Lake City: Deseret Book, 1979], p. 21.)

Marjorie Pay Hinckley is just one of the many women in the Church who have found real self-fulfillment in the pursuit of righteousness.

This individual pursuit of righteousness—her willingness to be molded by the Lord and His plan for her—has produced paradoxes and ironies. For instance, Marjorie Hinckley never published a book, and yet she has spent countless hours at a typewriter putting simple but powerful words to her thoughts and feelings. More often than not, the luxury of choosing those words carefully at a typewriter has been replaced with the necessity of finding them on her way to a pulpit. She has spoken effectively with and without interpreters in Church gatherings from the Tabernacle in Salt Lake City to the grand ballroom of the Seoul, Korea, Hyatt Hotel to Madison Square Garden in New

York City, and literally hundreds of other places in between. This little volume contains a fraction of those words—crafted and delivered to bless the lives of others.

Another irony is that Marjorie P. Hinckley never lived away from her parents' home until she married. With the exception of a few months in Denver, she has never lived outside Utah's Wasatch Front. And yet there is about her a universality. She is at home in the world. Her instant understanding reaches beyond the boundaries of age, economics, race, and nationality.

Family finances during the Depression precluded her graduating from college; she never wrote a master's thesis, never defended a dissertation. And yet she has been a lifelong learner who observes and reads voraciously, eagerly integrating and applying new knowledge.

She never learned to ride a bicycle and doesn't know how to swim, yet her adventures have not been ordinary. She has done missionary work in the resettlement flats of Hong Kong, shared a hotel room with lizards in Burma, walked along the Great Wall of China, and comforted near-starving babies in an orphanage in India.

She has never served as an officer of any corporation, never held political office of any kind, and never cashed a personal paycheck after the birth of her first child, yet her influence is profound. Traveling on every continent of the world, she has immediately established comfortable friendships with countless people. She has met and conversed easily with dignitaries and political leaders from a multitude of countries, from the queen of Thailand to the prime minister of England. She validates, inspires, and delights in every encounter.

Together with her husband of more than sixty years, President

Gordon B. Hinckley, she has reared five children. They have twenty-five grandchildren and twenty-four great-grandchildren. All of their children, grandchildren, and great-grandchildren adore her. She has blessed and continues to bless our lives in ways impossible to write. How can one describe the air one breathes?

Such are the strange and beautiful patterns the Lord weaves if we invite Him into our lives. This is a woman who eagerly allowed herself to become what the Lord needed her to be. She has been, from the very beginning, "packed shining and ready for whatever and when."

Mother would be the last person in the world to suggest that others should emulate her and her life. She, too, has had her opportunity to answer the questions: "What is this book?" and "Why publish it?" She resisted it with her own questions: "What *is* this, anyway?" and "Who, besides family, would *ever* want to read it?"

And so in answer to her and to the first question, "What?" I submit that this book is not a recipe for others to follow, but just one more example of the gospel in action in the life of a fellow sojourner. And to the final question, "Why publish it?" I respond with what I told Mother, that the gathering and the editing of the material had somehow changed me for the better, and that perhaps the book should be published with the hope that maybe, just maybe, we who read it will be inspired to try a little harder to be a little better—to become the people the Lord knows we can be. She reluctantly agreed, and we much less reluctantly offer you glimpses into the life and heart of a righteous woman.

Virginia H. Pearce
Salt Lake City, Utah

ACKNOWLEDGMENTS

*

There have been many who have provided encouragement as the compilation of this book went forward. Perhaps "persistent prodding" would be a more accurate description. Sheri Dew, vice president of publishing at Deseret Book, whom I love like a sister, had the tiresome duty of convincing us more than one time that the publishing of this book would be of positive value. She was ever cheerful and invaluable in soliciting and gathering writing from a multitude of sources. She made courageous attempts at educating and helping us do work that was far beyond our own abilities. Her secretary, Elsha Ulberg, is the perfect complement, always available and marvelously helpful.

A particular thanks to each contributor. Remembering and talking is one thing, but writing is a difficult discipline. We are grateful for the many generous contributions. Siblings, in-laws, children, grandchildren, and other family members are particularly appreciated for their willingness to share memories and insights. They also endured a fair amount of prodding and nagging. Their reluctance was not because they couldn't think of things to say but because they worried that they couldn't say them well enough to do this woman justice and that each page meant a little less privacy. I thank them for their generosity.

Sondra Grillone spent hours transcribing and entering material into the computer. Without her the entire mission would have been aborted early on. She worked accurately, quickly, and with enthusiasm.

Ron Millett, president of Deseret Book Company, and Kent Ware, director of publishing, have supported this project from the start. I thank them for their ongoing desire to bring uplifting books to the world. Thanks also to Emily Watts and those who work in editing and production at Deseret Book. Emily is not only thorough and skilled, she also laughs easily—a critical dimension during the course of this project. Thanks to Ron Stucki, designer, Patricia Parkinson, typographer, and others who worked hard to make the graphics reinforce the feeling and message of the book.

Thank you to my ever-patient husband and children, who have endured—once again—a preoccupied wife and mother who is perennially behind fast-approaching deadlines, and who behaves with so little grace under pressure.

It is a wonderful thing as a daughter to have parents who are loved by so many. I'd particularly like to thank the women of the Church who share my love for Marjorie Pay Hinckley. It is to her that the real acknowledgments and thanks belong.

C H A P T E R   O N E

FAITH

*

"I HAVE SEEN TOO MUCH TO EVER DENY IT"

Marjorie with her grandmother, Martha Elizabeth Paxman, 1912

1

President Harold B. Lee often said that our testimonies have to be reborn every day. I believe that is true. My testimony of this wonderful work grows every day. I know that God lives. I know He lives.

I have seen too much and experienced too much to ever deny it. He lives. He is truly my Father, and the Savior is my Savior in every sense of that word. If I can just be one more voice to say that God lives and that this is His work, I will be satisfied.

The faith of Marjorie P. Hinckley is simple and pure. Metaphysical mysteries have no place in her practical, bedrock belief in God and His work. Deep theological questions and discussions have never found a place in her conversation. But faith speaks through all of her actions and reactions.

Faith is the source of her personal sense of self-worth. The knowledge that she is in all reality a daughter of Heavenly Father gives her the dignity to move through life and give to others.

Faith is the foundation of her parenting techniques.

Faith is the wellspring of her unfailing support of her husband's single-minded devotion to the gospel.

Faith provides the warp against which hundreds and hundreds of personal friendships are woven.

Sister Hinckley's faith in God and His work extends to faith in others, as she gives them confidence in who they are and what they can become.

Her faith gives her an optimistic view of the future. Why wouldn't she feel excited about the future, when she really believes in God and His love for His people?

Her faith gives her an "other-centeredness," so that she sees her time and energy in terms of what she can do to further the righteous desires of those around her.

Her faith gives her a grateful heart and an appreciative word for everything and everyone. The wonders of life and blessings of heaven are evidence of God.

Her faith creates cheerfulness and a willingness to be flexible, to not overreact to daily irritations.

A common theme of her faith is the strength Sister Hinckley finds in her family and faithful ancestors. She is a fifth-generation member of the Church, having had ancestors who came across the plains during the pioneer period. She recounts their names and stories, not with any personal pride, but with tremendous gratitude. She draws real strength from their examples of fortitude, faith, and endurance.

Another prominent thread in the fabric of her faith is the contribution made to it as she observes the faithful lives of others. Tenderly told and retold stories of the testimonies of members whom she has met—from Hong Kong to

Auckland, from Europe to her own neighborhood—are included in virtually every talk she has ever given.

Sister Hinckley bears powerful and personal testimony of the prophets. She shares her up-close observations of these chosen men as evidence of her faith in the power of the restored church.

Faith is the life force behind the work necessary to fulfill her church callings and assignments. Over and over again she says, "I am a product of this church," as she talks about the power of participation in the kingdom of God. During her lifetime she has served as a ward Relief Society president, a ward Young Women president, and a ward Primary president, as well as in numerous stake leadership and teaching callings. She wears the title visiting teacher as comfortably as her own name.

Faith is Sister Hinckley's foundation. Her every virtue following faith will still be, first, last, and always, grounded in faith.

When we were very young, my mother used to read to us a lot. She read to us all kinds of books—from the classics to the stories of Jesus. There was a large picture that she had hung in our bedroom where my sisters and I slept. It was a picture that I know you are familiar with—the one of Jesus when He was twelve in the temple with the wise men. Every morning when I opened my eyes, the first thing I saw was the face of the young boy Jesus. I am grateful to my mother for many things that she did for us in a very subtle way. She didn't preach to us about Jesus, she just hung His picture where we could see it. I think that I was grown and long gone from the home before I realized what an impact that had on my life.

How I learned to love Him at a very young age! I still love Him, and every day I love Him more. I am grateful to have grown up in a family of faith, and I am grateful that my faith has never wavered.

Sister Patricia T. Holland, wife of Elder Jeffrey R. Holland of the Twelve, describes one of her first personal moments with Sister Hinckley— which was, at the same time, one of the most unsettling.

My husband was the relatively new president of Brigham Young University, and President Gordon B. Hinckley, then a counselor in the First Presidency, was to be the grand marshal of the annual BYU Homecoming Parade. We had not yet had much experience at the university, and had had almost no personal experiences with the Hinckleys. We invited them down to the President's Home for a light breakfast before going to the midmorning parade.

Sometime prior to the start of the parade, the Church security man who was escorting President Hinckley received a telephone call that there might be some difficulty. A man known to have some mental and emotional instability was apparently in Provo for the festivities and had made some irrational remarks to a friend about what he might do during the parade. Without being overly dramatic, I will just say that his plans involved the safety of President Hinckley and my husband. The one who heard the comments was concerned enough to contact the local police, and the police contacted Church Security.

When the report came in, I was beside myself. I always worry about the safety of everyone anyway, and this sounded serious to me! The best way I can describe President Hinckley's reaction is to say he was amused. But my husband and the other officials immediately put precautions in place as befitting the safety of a member of the First Presidency. Soon I could see (or thought I could see!)

Church Security men, BYU police, and Provo City police under every bush and in every tree. But the thing that most astonished me through all of this was how calm Sister Hinckley was. With everyone scurrying here and there, she just kept smiling that adorable smile of hers, said, "It will be all right," and kept on reading her book.

Well, everything *was* all right, and the morning went forward without an interruption or difficulty of any kind. But, of course, I didn't know it was going to go that well at the time. I later told Sister Hinckley how impressed I was at her calm and soothing manner through what seemed to me to be a very serious moment for our husbands. She said, "Pat, I learned a long time ago that this is the Lord's work and these brethren are the Lord's servants. They have to be wise and careful, but in the end they are in the Lord's hands. I stopped worrying about Gordon a long time ago because I knew it couldn't do much good. I just pray for him, ask him to be careful, and trust that the Lord knows every situation we are in."

I have never forgotten that early moment with Sister Hinckley, a moment now reinforced by nearly two additional decades of close, tender, and delightful times with her. That sweet, calm smile, that unruffled manner, and above all that pure, perfect faith is the Marjorie Hinckley all the wives of the General Authorities have come to love and admire. Nothing seems to unnerve her, and nothing seems too great for her to face or overcome. I said something to her about what challenging and demanding lives they had—going so many places, doing so many things, being tired almost beyond description even as the years keep adding up. She just smiled that smile of hers and said, "It is difficult sometimes, Pat, but it still isn't as hard as crossing the plains." Ever the modest one, ever the self-effacing, humble one, ever the one to make any circumstance more bearable with that smile, a little humor, and unwavering faith that "It will be all right."

When I was a mother with young children, we had a monthly leadership meeting on Thursday nights. On one particular Thursday I was tired. I had children to get to bed and dishes to wash. I did not want to go to the meeting. But I went.

When the recently called stake president stood up, the first thing he said was, "Brothers and sisters, Joseph Smith either had a vision or he didn't." He said that he didn't know what he could say to encourage us in our efforts other than the fact that Joseph Smith either had a vision or he didn't. If he did not, then we were engaged in a tremendous hoax, but if he did, then it behooved each of us to give all the time, money, effort, and energy we could muster to promote the kingdom of God.

That is all it took to remind me that this is the work of the Lord, and the most important thing we can do is to serve in every way we can. I have recalled this stake president's words many times, particularly when I have thought that perhaps the Church requires too much of my time and energy.

I am grateful for the testimony that I have that Joseph Smith did have a vision. I am grateful that he found it in his heart to take his anxieties to the Lord in prayer. Otherwise, I would be barren of all the spiritual blessings I enjoy.

Elder Bruce Hafen, when presenting Sister Hinckley with BYU's Exemplary Womanhood Award in 1996, said this of her:

Sister Hinckley's entire life is a study in spiritual strength. Her faith is practical, honest, and it runs very deep, anchored in strong roots planted by her pioneer forebears. She has said she can't "remember a time when our five children were growing up that their father was able to sit with us in church." Yet her children cannot remember ever once hearing their mother complain about the relentless demands the Church has made on their family. One of the secrets of this happy marriage is that President and Sister Hinckley have instinctively seen the gospel, the Church, their marriage, and their family life all as part of a single, bedrock commitment to following the Lord's way.

In almost every message Sister Hinckley has ever given from a pulpit, she has talked about testimony. It is not only a beginning point for her but something to think about and build on daily.

"[Jesus] saith unto them, But whom say ye that I am?

"And Simon Peter answered and said, Thou art the Christ, the Son of the living God.

"And Jesus answered and said unto him, Blessed art thou, Simon Bar-jona: for flesh and blood hath not revealed it unto thee, but my Father which is in heaven" (Matthew 16:15–17).

Surely a testimony is something that we cannot get in any other way. We must get it through the Holy Ghost. If one person could give it to another, all parents who possessed it would give it to their children. It cannot be bought with money. It can be had only when we have made ourselves worthy and have sought the Lord in humility and diligence. Then it will surely be ours.

Expressions of confidence and faith in the future are a constant in her correspondence with family members and friends:

March 3, 1985

Dear Ones,

Dad talked with you this morning and we gather that these are rather stressful days for you, but even this will pass away and the lessons learned will be a future blessing. There are some years in our lives that we would not want to live again.

"Be patient in afflictions, for thou shalt have many; but endure them, for, lo, I am with thee, even unto the end of thy days" (D&C 24:8).

End of sermon.

You are loved.

M.

*****

We have been thinking a lot of the trials and tribulations of _____. If the Lord chastises those he loves, she is greatly loved. She is learning some hard lessons of life at a very tender age. It may not seem ideal, but somehow, some way, things will work out and we will all rejoice with her. She is such a talented and outstanding girl. You will have to buy that little card for her that says:

"When the going gets tough,

The tough get going."

Just tell her to hang tight and do her best.

That is my lecture for today.

XOXOXOXO,

M.

*****

Dear, darling, wonderful Amy,

Another Christmas has come and gone. December is a wonderful month. The spirit of Christmas hovers over everyone and everything. Everyone seems just a little kinder, more gentle, and more loving.

We are having a great time. Grandpa loves to get out with the people and is determined to go 'til he drops. He is blessed with good health. We both are, and what a blessing that is! We are headed for Mexico in a few weeks and then to Africa. What a great church to belong to! And besides that, it is true.

Every day brings its own challenges, as you well know, but life would be a total waste without knowing what it is all about.

How we love you! And are so proud of you.

Grandma Hinckley.

Family letters—full of the news and details of life—often end with a little postscript affirming faith. To a granddaughter away at college, Sister Hinckley wrote:

I just balanced my checkbook and had $20.00 left over. Spend it on something useful—like food, clothing, or shelter.

Love,

Grandma H.

P.S. Keep the faith. It pays such great dividends!

A letter dated December 1980 ended with another typical postscript:

P.S. We are anxiously waiting for something wonderful to happen to you and have faith that it will. After all, 1981 is a new year.

One of Sister Hinckley's sons recalls his mother's everyday kind of faith:

Like most of us, Mother has a few phobias, fears based on some fact and much uncertainty. One of these phobias is water—especially deep water. Actually, anything more than about six inches of water, she considers deep water.

Many years ago, Dad had been asked by the Moyle family to finish the biography of their grandfather, James Henry Moyle. He was working full days at the office, and so he tried to get into this project during the evenings and on Saturdays. The task was too big, so he decided to devote some vacation time to the project. He took a week off—it might have been two—and stayed home, his typewriter on the table surrounded by research materials.

It was summertime, and we children were having our usual good times, playing with friends and charging around. One day he stood up from the table and said, "How can I write a book with you kids running in and out of the house from morning to night making a racket?" He came up with a wonderful solution: for the remainder of his vacation, he would rent a cabin in nearby Big Cottonwood Canyon, where Mother and we children would live. He would stay at home in East Millcreek and write. We thought it was a splendid plan.

After breakfast on the first morning, Mother told us that we were going on a hike to Twin Lakes. We packed a picnic lunch and off we went, all of us in high spirits, and Mother in her pedal pushers.

We hiked to the lake. Then about three-quarters of the way around the lake the trail became steep as it turned from the woods down toward the edge of the lake. The trail was lined with brush and small trees, so that there was no other route. The lake looked quite deep even at its edge—dark and still—and it did in fact look as though, if we were not careful, we could slide right into the lake and sink from sight in its frigid waters before the narrow trail turned to the right along the shoreline.

Mother's aquaphobia struck with a vengeance, causing her to freeze with terror. Here we were, with the choice of going forward or retreating miles the way we had come. Suddenly she said, "We forgot to have family prayers this morning!" So she gathered us around, and we knelt on the ground, supporting our elbows on a fallen log, and had a prayer—with the very specific plea that we might get through this impasse without falling into the water. When we stood up we knew we would make it. And what's more, we were sure that, even with Mother's aquaphobia, she now knew we would make it. We proceeded cautiously, sitting down and sliding the last few feet until all of us were safely around the turn and past the water's edge.

We are His children, and if we ever got that through our heads thoroughly, understood that completely, we would never do a small thing, we would never say a cross word, we would not use bad language, we would not criticize anybody, we would love everyone the way the Savior loves us.

A sister, Evelyn P. Henriksen, says.

We have a loving, faithful family. When adversity comes into one of our lives, Marjorie always says, "There is a lot of faith in this family. We will pray us through this one." Whenever I personally have any kind of difficulty, I call my sister for advice, comfort, understanding, encouragement, and most of all a reassurance of faith.

A wellspring of Marjorie's faith is her reverence and love for her ances-
tors. Heather B. Blair, a granddaughter, recalls being blessed by this love:

Grandma Hinckley has a great love for her ancestors. As a
young child I was fascinated with the papers, pictures, and pedigree
charts that frequently covered the dining-room table at Grandma's
house. Rather than shooing me away and telling me that I was too
young, Grandma taught me everything she knew about family history. She even purchased a book of remembrance for me and helped
me get started on my own family history. She would take me to the
genealogical library with her. I loved when summer came and I
could spend all day doing family history with Grandma. She helped
me to have a great love for my heritage and to get to know my
ancestors personally.

I wear a simple gold band on my finger. It's 18-karat gold and
is over a hundred years old. It belonged to my Grandmother
Paxman. She told me a story—more than once—about it when
I was young. She was widowed at the age of twenty-two, and this
was her wedding ring. She never remarried, and the ring was precious to her because it was all she had left to remind her of her
young husband. One day she was changing the straw in the mat-
tress, which she did yearly. She lost the ring. The story goes that
she felt desperate at the loss and prayed. Then she looked down
on the ground, and there was the ring. Her story convinced me
that prayers are heard and that prayers are answered.

The inspiring stories of Sister Hinckley's ancestors are sprinkled through-
out her gospel talks. Her purpose in repeating them often is to encourage an

increase in faith. The following is excerpted from a published article she wrote ("Music Was the Missionary," Ensign, July 1981, p. 48):

"On a beautiful Sunday morning in the fall of 1841, my great-grandfather, William Minshall Evans, then sixteen years of age, was walking down the streets of Liverpool, England, on his way to church. Suddenly he heard singing that thrilled him beyond anything he had ever heard before. He followed the sound down an alley and up some rickety stairs into a room where a few people were holding a meeting. John Taylor, who later became president of the Church and who had a beautiful tenor voice, was the singer. The song he sang was so beautiful that William remained to hear the sermon.

"Upon returning home, William was reprimanded by his elder brother, David, for being absent from the accustomed place in the choir. Asked to give an account of himself, William replied, 'I have been where you should have been, and I shall not be satisfied until you all hear the wonderful truth I have heard this morning.'

" . . . William and David were converted to the gospel, and then helped convert other members of their family. . . .

"I never sing the hymns of the Church without remembering that it was the singing of a hymn that opened the door to the gospel for my family and made it possible for me to enjoy all the blessings that have followed."

Faith-building pioneer stories were a part of her heritage from her earliest childhood:

Each 24th of July during my growing-up years my father would take all of us children up to Little Mountain in Emigration

Canyon, to the place where the pioneers came over the hill into the Salt Lake Valley. We would sit on the rocks while he told us the story of his mother, Mary Goble Pay, and the suffering she experienced as part of the ill-fated Martin handcart company, who were caught in early winter storms as they made their way to join the Saints in Zion.

Father did not moralize or lecture, but the love and appreciation he had for his mother's faith and courage was transferred to our young, impressionable hearts. It was while I was still very young that I made up my mind I would stay true and faithful to the gospel so her suffering would not be in vain. Although she died when I was just six months old, I knew that the day would come when I would see her again. How could I face her if I had not built on the foundation she had laid?

Laura P. Jenkins, a granddaughter, describes how a gift from her grandmother created within her a resolve to be faithful and to instill faith in her children:

When each of the granddaughters is married, Grandma gives us a priceless treasure. It is a framed collection of portraits showing seven generations on our maternal line, back to the first woman on that line who accepted the gospel in Cambridge, England. They are: Sarah Jarold Hyder (1800–1897); her daughter, Charlotte Hyder Evans (1834–1906); her daughter, Martha Elizabeth Evans Paxman (1866–1954); her daughter, Georgetta Paxman Pay (1888–1980); her daughter, Marjorie Pay Hinckley (1911–); in my case, her daughter, Virginia Hinckley Pearce (1945–); and then a portrait taken at

14

Four generations of Hinckley women

the time of my marriage, Laura Pearce Jenkins (1969–). Along with the framed portraits are short laminated biographies of each woman, written by Grandma.

Recently, my cousin Celia and I were at the Women's Conference in Provo. We had been to a few classes that were hopefully going to make us wonderful mothers who would rear incredibly talented, bright, and faithful children. We noted the accomplishments of the panelists and their parenting strengths. We began discussing what our children will think of us when they look back. Will they say, "My mother was a great pianist who brought a love for music into our home"? Well, that wasn't it. Will they say, "She was incredibly bright and a gifted teacher at home and in her profession"? or "She was uniquely creative. Mom could make a fun experiment out of anything"? No to both of those.

Later that evening, we went to visit my sister in Orem. She pulled out two beautiful Easter dresses she had made with smocking and ribbon embroidery, along with an exquisite blessing dress she was sewing for her new baby daughter. Celia and I looked at each other. Well, our children would definitely not look back and call us seamstresses. But we kept thinking. It would be so nice to decide on that one special thing now, so that we could focus on it while rearing our children. But we couldn't come up with anything that seemed to fit our personalities and that seemed to come quite naturally.

I continued to think about this dilemma until one day I glanced at Grandma's gift hanging on my wall. I sat down with the little biographies and reread them carefully. Each woman had special gifts and talents, but I began to notice a strong golden thread—a thread repeated over and over as Grandma recorded the lives of those good women. Every one of them was full of faith. Every one had made and kept temple covenants.

Suddenly I had my answer. If I could choose only one thing for my children, I would want them to develop faith in our Heavenly Father. I want my children to say that their mother was a faithful member of the Church who kept her covenants. I want to show them by example how to be faithful themselves. I want them and their children to become part of the legacy of faith that Grandma has given to me.

When I made this startling discovery, I wrote to my sister, who was serving a mission. She wrote back enthusiastically: "You're right, Laura. We may be duds, but we can be faithful duds!"

We certainly can. Thanks for the gift, Grandma.

We have our work cut out for us. We have a very important role to play in the building up of God's kingdom. We do not have to walk the dusty plains and live in undesirable dwellings and fight off mobs and hostile Indians, but we have our own little battles to fight.

Sometime before her marriage, Marjorie Pay shared these thoughts in a stake conference talk:

Emerson expresses a majestic thought when he says: "It is easy in the world to live after the world's opinion; it is easy in solitude to live after our own; but the great man is he who in the midst of the crowd keeps with perfect sweetness the independence of solitude."

If there is one fundamental doctrine in Mormonism it is that man is an individual created in the likeness of God, with divinely bestowed free agency, and that the development of the human individual soul is so important a thing that God himself has called it His greatest work and glory.

The foundation of faith and testimony is action. Sister Hinckley reminds us that the way to increase our testimony is to keep the commandments.

How can we know if this gospel is a thing of God if we do not do the works of God? Have you ever noticed that the people who say they do not have testimonies and who are inclined to scoff at the things of God are usually people who are not trying out religion by living the laws and commandments? The only way we can know whether or not this is the true church is to try it out for ourselves. Until we have given it a fair chance, we are hardly in a position to pass judgment. We will come to know that the gospel is true by trying it out.

In 1958 the Hinckleys traveled to New Zealand for the dedication of the temple. They stayed in the home of the temple president along with President and Sister David O. McKay. It was Marjorie's first opportunity to associate with a Church president in an informal setting. Her remembrances of that time are a reflection of her faith:

I got to see what President McKay was like, whether he liked cold pie or hot pie, so to speak. And it was wonderful. I would sit across the dining-room table after we had eaten and just revel in the experience of being with a prophet. President McKay had an aura about him that was simply overpowering.

Through my experiences I have come to the sure knowledge in my own mind that President McKay is a prophet of God, that when he stretched out his hand and placed temples in Los Angeles, Switzerland, London, and faraway New Zealand, the Lord had spoken again that the kingdom of God might flourish and fill the earth.

President McKay was described at the New Zealand Temple dedication as a great torchlight striding through the earth lighting the lamps of truth. Your candle has been lighted; mine has been lighted; it is up to us to keep the flame flickering and thereby light many more.

Marjorie Hinckley has attended dozens of temple dedications. She always reports them as cherished spiritual experiences. The dedications of the Swiss, New Zealand, and London Temples were particularly memorable for her because her husband had special responsibilities, and therefore they spent several weeks preceding the dedications getting things ready for the dedications as well as the operation of the temples.

She reports a time of reflection one evening prior to the London Temple dedication.

During the London Temple open house preceding the dedication, we took a day off to spend some time in Preston, a rather gray industrial town north of London where my husband had labored as a young missionary. We were late coming home, and as we got off the bus we walked through the grounds. The sweet strains of the Tabernacle Choir singing "O My Father" were coming from speakers hidden in the huge oak trees. "Lovely, isn't it," my husband said. Lovely?! It was just like walking into heaven! Never before in my life was I so thankful for the gospel as I was at that moment. I didn't wonder anymore why people lined up for two and three blocks to visit this spot. It wasn't to see the beautiful grounds. It was because what they found there was peace and goodwill and the spirit of truth and light.

The light of Christ brings peace to the troubled mind, rest to the weary, solace to those in sorrow, and joy to those who walk uprightly.

Testimony is the structural foundation for lifelong faith. Each individual must gain and continue to nourish his or her own personal testimony, as Sister Hinckley attests:

I remember a time in my life when I didn't want to lean on anyone else's testimony. I wanted it to be mine. Everybody has to come to it on his own. I was probably seventeen then. I took that problem to the Lord and I got it solved. I have faith. I do. I have a lot of faith.

James Pearce, a grandson, recalls an afternoon visit with his grandmother:

Just before I left on my mission, I was downtown doing errands and decided to drop by and see Grandma. Just like always, she was delighted to see me. She told me how great I was and how proud she was that I was going on a mission. The best parts of the conversation, and the parts I keep thinking about, were her little testimony "bytes"—just one-liners that are the everyday way she keeps telling you how much she believes. Sentences like:

"Wouldn't life be terrible without the gospel?"

"It wouldn't be worth the hassle; really it wouldn't."

"If it weren't for the gospel we just couldn't face it."

"There is so much of hardness to face that if it weren't for the gospel I don't know what would become of us."

Common-sense advice is often wrapped inside the testimony sandwiches:

"Remember, James, that the Lord needs healthy missionaries. Take care of your health. Get enough sleep and eat right."

And then another testimony slice:

"The gospel's true."

"I'm sure you know that as well as I do."

"I've seen too much and experienced too much in my life to ever deny it."

"Everyone needs the gospel."

I think about her testimony every time I teach investigators. She's right. *Everyone* needs the gospel. How *does* anyone live without it?

Jodi Hinckley, a granddaughter, also remembers her grandmother's strong testimony:

One weekend near Easter, Grandma and Grandpa took a few of us [granddaughters] to St. George. In the morning, at around 8:00 A.M., when Grandpa had eaten breakfast and awakened us all with his whistling, saying the day was "practically over," Grandma sat us all down at the table and read the story of the Resurrection to us out of the scriptures.

It was a very powerful experience for me—one that I will never forget. Not only did I feel the Spirit strongly, but I was able to see Grandma's testimony shine through her as she told us of the

Atonement. It is a very important thing to see someone you love and respect so much share her testimony with you on an intimate basis.

Sister Hinckley consistently saw her opportunities to travel with the president of the Church as faith-promoting and learning experiences. She describes some of the experiences she had with President and Sister Harold B. Lee:

We went on two separate occasions with President and Sister Lee to England, Germany, Austria, Italy, Greece, and the Holy Land, where we met with missionaries, members, youth, and servicemen.

Never did anyone have more gracious, more courteous, more kind traveling companions. It was interesting to see how President Lee moved into a situation. When we met with the missionaries, it was usually in the morning in a chapel filled with full-time and part-time local missionaries. As he stood to address them, he would seldom start with a word of greeting or preliminary remarks but would open the scriptures and begin a discourse. He moved through the scriptures with such ease that sometimes it was difficult to know when the words were his and when he was quoting. After one such meeting I asked him how he had gone about memorizing the scriptures. Did he follow a program of memorizing one a day, or how had he accomplished this? He thought for a moment and then said, "I don't think I ever consciously memorized a scripture. I guess I have just worked them through so much that they have become a part of me and my vocabulary."

We were in England one Sunday. It had been a full day: two

sessions of a conference and a fireside at night. When we got back to the hotel about 9:30, we were bone-weary and hungry. We went into the hotel dining room to get a little something to eat. The day was over—we could relax. At least, that is what I thought. The next thing I knew, the waitress had her pencil poised to write down our order. President Lee looked up at her and said, "What church do you belong to?" The day was not over for him. He had embarked on a proselyting exercise. Before the meal was over he had learned all about this young woman. She had lost her husband and was lonely and afraid. She had promised to see the missionaries and learn more. It was a beautiful thing to see the president of the Church practice what he had been preaching all that day. When the waitress (a woman of perhaps thirty-five) learned that the man she was talking with was the president, the prophet, seer, and revelator of the Church of Jesus Christ, she could not believe that such a person would stoop to making conversation with such a one as she. She was greatly moved.

For years the Church had been trying to get into Greece to preach the gospel to those wonderful people. The doors were closed to us. Brother Hinckley at this particular time had already made two trips there, together with others, but all in vain. Now President Lee himself had come. This time it would happen. I was sure of it. After all, hadn't the prophet himself come with fasting and with prayer? At the end of a long and frustrating day, the door to Greece was still closed. I was crushed, disappointed, shocked. "Aren't you discouraged?" I asked. President Lee replied, "No, I am not discouraged. All this means is that it is not yet the Lord's time to open the work in Greece." Then he went on to explain that they had to keep trying, so that when the Lord's time had come to open the work, we would be there knocking on the door. I learned a great lesson from that.

I cannot talk about President Lee without saying something about Sister Lee. She is a woman so warm, so gracious, so caring that everyone's problems become her problems. She is at home with the mayor of Jerusalem, the taxicab driver, or the boy who delivers her paper.

Everywhere he went, President Lee received the adulation of the people. Fathers would hold their children on their shoulders that they might get a better look at the prophet. Mothers made their way through crowds to have him kiss their babies. I always had the feeling that this made him uncomfortable. In his talks to the people he would say over and over, "This is not my church. I am only a man. This church belongs to the Lord, Jesus Christ." On one occasion he said, "I am only a man who has squatters' rights here for a short time." Three months later he was gone.

But the things I learned from him will never leave me.

Though she has had unusual and wonderful opportunities to learn from prophets, Sister Hinckley also has a practical, everyday dimension to her faith. She spoke to young adult women about this kind of faith:

There is something about spirituality that is central to the life of a woman.

I do not mean the kind of spirituality that only takes you to church on Sunday. Sitting in church will not necessarily make you into a Christian anymore than sitting in a garage will make you into a car. I am talking about the kind of spirituality that makes you behave like a child of God.

I am talking about the kind of spirituality that breathes reverence into every act and deed.

I am talking about the spirituality that makes you loving and grateful, and forgiving, and patient, and gentle, and long-suffering with that roommate who drops her clothes on the closet floor and who never, no never, does her share of the cooking and cleaning and who does not ask you before borrowing your pen for the day and who beat you to the boyfriend.

I am talking about the kind of spirituality that compels you to get in touch with your Heavenly Father every single day of your life.

Sister Hinckley's love for the missionaries is an expression of her faith:

Walking into a chapel filled with missionaries is like walking into a room charged with electricity. The power of the priesthood is magnified in these young men to such an extent that it is a miracle to watch them perform.

Back in 1960, when the work was started in the Philippines, we accompanied four elders being transferred from Hong Kong to this new area. In my eyes they were just boys, nineteen and twenty years old—simple, unlearned in the ways of the world. I thought of my boy at home, just turning nineteen. I would hardly trust him to buy the weekend groceries, and here were four such young men with the overwhelming responsibility of establishing the kingdom of God in the Philippine Islands.

When we were leaving the country I looked at those four missionaries—just a handful of members and no other missionaries in the entire country—and I said to my husband, "How can you leave those four boys there alone?" And he said, "They're not alone. The Lord is with them."

He proved to be right. The Lord was with them. When we returned six months later there were thirteen good, solid members meeting in the living room of the elders' quarters. Then there were seventy-five members and they rented the Masonic Lodge. Fourteen years later we had the glorious experience of attending the area conference in Manila. Some 18,000 people attended, the largest area conference ever held anywhere in the world, at that date. A miracle.

Eighteen thousand people seems like just a number, but it means 18,000 lives that have taken on new meaning. And I thought of my husband's words about those four young missionaries: "They're not alone. The Lord is with them."

A postcard to a two-year-old grandson, written from Laie, Hawaii, is a simple expression of her enthusiasm for missionary work:

Dear Spencer,

There are many, many missionaries on this island. Last year they baptized enough people for two new stakes.

I hope you will be a missionary someday.
Love,
Grandma Hinckley

Evelyn P. Henriksen describes her sister's love of missionary work:

There is no question how important missions and missionaries are to Marjorie. I'll never forget when their first son, Richard, received his mission call. At his farewell she said that as involved as she and Gordon had been with missions and missionaries throughout the years, she could now finally say she was a missionary mother.

Many years later, when my husband and I received a call to serve in Fiji, she said, "Evelyn, I am so excited for you both. However, you must realize you will need to be my close informant because we will never have the opportunity to serve this way."

I was touched that now we would be able to tell her our feelings—directly from the field. Consequently, we sent her a copy of our weekly family letters so she could share in our experiences. She always let us know of her approval, her love, and her interest.

Her service, of course, was to be an influence with the thousands of missionaries and their presidents. Very often when she would return home from a mission tour she would telephone the parents of missionaries she had met. She loved doing this, and the parents were always surprised and touched.

Sister Hinckley's description of President and Sister Spencer W. Kimball serves as an expression of her testimony. Her admiration of President Kimball's relentless work style gives us a glimpse of her own belief—that when you know the Church is true, there is no such thing as working too hard.

The most impressive thing about President Kimball was his indomitable will to get the work done. His energy and his unrelenting drive made traveling with him something less than relaxed. We went with him to the Washington Temple, then to the London Temple, and then on an all-night flight to South

Africa for an area conference. From there an all-night flight across the Atlantic to South America. Three more area conferences and the dedication of the São Paulo Temple. For what seemed like endless days we were riding planes, climbing on and off buses, sitting in long meetings. Some of us got tired, but what can one say when the President was the first one in the hotel lobby every morning with a cheery "Did you rest well last night?"

At the end of the three days of dedication at the São Paulo Temple, and with the area conference beginning there the next morning, President Kimball decided he wanted to meet with all the missionaries at 7:30 that night in the São Paulo chapel. His doctor said "No." Bear in mind that during those nine sessions of the dedication, three sessions a day for three days, he had been on his feet speaking for close to three hours a day. Others tried to dissuade him, but he was firm. He would meet with the missionaries. Many of those in the party went back to their hotels, weary, but we decided to board the bus and go with the President where 1100 missionaries had gathered: full-time missionaries, local missionaries, returned missionaries, prospective missionaries.

There were 1100 of them, yet he talked to them as if he were talking with each one in the privacy of his living room. He spoke without notes, from his heart. It was a talk that will never be published in the *Ensign* or any other place, but I took notes as fast as I could write, and I love occasionally to read them over. They are so typically President Kimball.

He talked to the missionaries about nothing being impossible with the Lord. He talked to them about the charge we have to convert the world. He said, "In every land the people are great, and it is going to be a monstrous job to teach them. But the Lord was not joking when he said, 'Go ye into all the world and teach every creature.'"

And then he elaborated by saying, "Nothing is impossible to God. An angel announced to Sarah something that was impossible. She laughed. The angel said, 'Why did you laugh?' She said, 'I didn't laugh.' He said, 'You did. But whether you laugh or not, you will have a son.'"

And many other things did he say to them. "The day will come when the Lord will say, 'The work is finished.' Temples will dot the land. All will be paying tithing. All young men will go on missions. And then we will say: 'Isn't it wonderful. Look what has been done.'"

Then when we thought he was finished, in typical style he turned to the brethren seated behind him and said, "Can I have just one more minute?"

He went on to say: "People say, 'How can you shake hands with so many people?' I explain that I milked cows all my growing-up years, so that my hands would be strong to shake hands. I wrote out the Articles of Faith and put them down on the ground on the left-hand side of the milk stool and I memorized the Articles of Faith. You can do it. The Lord will help you, and you can do it easier now than when you are eighty-three!"

It was a wonderful hour. I think every missionary there will remember it forever.

Sister Kimball was one of the most noble women ever born into this world. She was bright, brilliant, dignified, always warm and loving. Always smiling. Never complaining. She had her health problems too, but whenever you

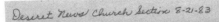

Photo by Owen Stayner

Susan Rahimzadeh and Tony Slagle greet Camilla E. Kimball, middle, and Marjorie P. Hinckley at Primary commemoration.

28

asked how she was feeling, she only laughed. I often wondered what the laugh covered up.

Steven C. Bennion, a neighbor, describes Sister Hinckley's commitment to her own Church callings, even after her support of her husband's calling required much of her time.

After her husband was called as a General Authority and then a member of the Council of the Twelve just three years later, Sister Hinckley continued to give very important service in her home ward. My sister Ellen was a new Laurel in the ward when Sister Hinckley was called as the Laurel adviser in the late 1960s. Ellen was tall, bright, and, at the time, somewhat shy. Ellen said that every lesson taught by Sister Hinckley was uplifting and stimulating, and caused her to think deeply about important things. It was indeed a special window in a young woman's life that made a major difference to her. Marjorie Hinckley was often involved in trips with her husband to the Orient and elsewhere, yet she still took the time to make a major difference in the lives of people in her own ward and neighborhood.

One daughter describes her mother's dedication to Church work:

I was a little freckled ten-year-old, sitting at the dining-room table helping my mother get ready for her Primary leadership meeting. She was the stake leader for the Seagulls [the eleven-year-old Primary girls] and it was her job to arrive that night with posters and enrichment material that the ward Seagull teachers would use during the coming month. So we were cutting out four or five of everything. I got to choose the people for the posters, cutting them out of the array of old sewing pattern envelopes before me. Each poster began with a little girl and ended up with a mature woman. Each was attached to some kind of string. At the end of each string was the appropriate phrase: "Thoughts become words, words become actions, actions become habits, habits become character, and character is what we really are." The first little person held a thread, the next dental floss, the next a string, the next heavy twine, and the last a piece of rope. I've never forgotten the poster or the message.

My parents taught the gospel mostly by example, but the actual talking about gospel principles often happened in the context of mother's Church callings.

The dining-room table would sprout more and more books and papers each day as her Relief Society lesson approached. She would sometimes be studying when I came in from school—so excited about the material that she was a magnet for my attention. I shuffled through her notes and posters and I absorbed it all. Most of all, I absorbed in a deep, deep place her love of Church work. It's where I saw her mind and heart come alive with all of her immense talents focused on the lesson or event of the week.

When I was in high school she was the ward Relief Society president. I remember that year because, unlike most of my life, I would often come home to an empty house. I knew where Mother was. Our ward stretched from 2700 East to the top of Mill Creek Canyon. There was a couple who were the caretakers at Tracy Wigwam Boy Scout Camp up the canyon. The wife had cancer of the stomach, and Mother was her Relief Society president. I was always a little deflated to come home from school to an empty house, but that feeling quickly evaporated against what I felt as I watched my mother on those days when she had been taking care of her Relief Society sister. She would come home so sad and so full of pure love—describing the terrible tumor growing larger and larger, and this woman's courage.

The sister died that year. I never met her. Now that I think of it, I wonder why. Was she a member? Was she less active? Maybe they couldn't leave their post to attend meetings. Maybe she was quiet, and I just had never noticed her at church. I don't know, but even her invisibility was a powerful testimony to me of Relief Society compassion. Had she been mother's best friend, perhaps the lesson of gospel service wouldn't have been so sweet.

I love Church work. Is it any wonder, with a mother like that?

Sister Hinckley comments on the opportunity for service provided within the structure of the Church:

How simple it is, really, to extend a kindness when we see the need. Jesus set the example on many occasions. An example I love is when the scriptures said that He led the blind man out of the town. Just a small kindness, but a powerful example. God help us to recognize the opportunities we have when we participate in the organizations of the Church.

One fall afternoon Brother Hinckley and I stepped off a plane in Athens, Greece. At the airport to meet us was a Latter-day Saint woman and her husband from Idaho who were on a two-year teaching assignment in Athens. (The Church was not officially recognized or organized in Greece at the time.) We explained to them that we would be there only about twenty hours and inquired if there was anything that they needed or anything that we could do for them.

The sister spoke up and said, "Couldn't we just hold a Latter-day Saint meeting: have a prayer, sing the songs of Zion, and have some talks?" So that night we met in their apartment. They invited three well-dressed Indian women and two young American men. We sat in a circle and began the meeting.

Just an ordinary Latter-day Saint meeting. We sang, "We Thank Thee, O God, for a Prophet." Then an opening prayer was offered. We sang another hymn, and it was then that I noticed the tears welling up in my new friend's eyes. She leaned over to me and said, "Oh, you'll just have to pardon me. You don't know how wonderful it feels just to be sitting in a Latter-day Saint meeting. I miss it so much."

Since then, each time I sit in a Latter-day Saint meeting, whether it be a sacrament meeting, a Relief Society meeting, a leadership meeting, or a Sunday School class, I say a quiet prayer to my Heavenly Father, thanking him for just being able to meet with my friends, in the name of the Lord.

If the Lord wanted to punish me, I can think of nothing that would hurt me more than to be denied the privilege of meeting with the members of The Church of Jesus Christ of Latter-day Saints.

Of particular importance to Sister Hinckley is sacrament meeting:

It is one thing to talk to a Relief Society group or an MIA [Young Women] class or a fireside, but it is something else again to speak in a sacrament meeting. I feel completely unnerved. Perhaps this is because of the solemnness and sacredness of a sacrament meeting. It is different from any other meeting held in the Church.

When President Ezra Taft Benson was the president of the Church, he challenged the Saints to read and reread the Book of Mormon. Sister Hinckley shares several experiences with that counsel:

"Feast upon the words of Christ." I love the word "feast." We talk about "pondering" the scriptures, but I like the phrase "feast upon the words."

It is interesting that President Benson's big thrust has been to get us back to reading the Book of Mormon on a continuing basis. And the response has been tremendous. Letters have poured in, dozens of cards, a huge poster with hundreds of signatures of people who have answered the clarion call and have read or reread the Book of Mormon. Many say that their lives have been changed, some turned completely around. Not only adults responded, but children and teenagers. We were in Cody, Wyoming, about six weeks ago. The stake Primary president gave us a huge glass jar filled with jelly beans to bring home to President Benson. For every chapter in the Book of Mormon a Primary child read, the child placed a jelly bean in the jar. One little girl of ten proudly told us that she had read every single chapter.

A knock came at our door about two weeks ago, and there stood my wonderful eighty-four-year-old neighbor with her granddaughter from California, whom she wanted us to meet. This little girl was eight years old. She had red hair and freckles and an adorable smile. She had accomplished her goal to read the entire Book of Mormon before her baptism. Phenomenal!

A university coed who has had a very busy summer has been through the Book of Mormon four times in the last five months. The first time she marked every reference to or word of Jesus Christ in red. The second time she underlined all the doctrine in blue. Then all the references to records and record keeping in black, and finally all the history underlined in green. And this was a girl who a year ago was saying, "It seems like all President Benson is saying is read the Book of Mormon, read the Book of Mormon." But when she decided to be obedient, she went all out. Now she has me marking a new Book of Mormon in her suggested colors.

Wonderful things are happening, and I can think of nothing better President Benson could do for the members than to get us involved in an extraordinary way with this tremendous book of scripture.

Our young people need this to safely steer them through the very wicked world they are being tossed around in.

We hear continually what a wicked world this is, and what a terrible world it is for children to grow up in. Perhaps that is why so much emphasis is being placed on scripture reading. I firmly believe that this is one thing that is going to save the present generation of young people. And I don't feel unduly concerned about them. I don't know when there has ever been a generation when the young have been so involved in the scriptures. It was not so in my day. We heard much about tithing and about the Word of Wisdom but very little about scripture reading.

Primary lessons and sharing time revolve around the scriptures—not just stories, but children are becoming acquainted with the actual words.

But scriptures are not just for the young. Scriptures are needed more and more as the years rush by. They become more and more meaningful because we have more and more experiences that help us to relate to them.

Marjorie Hinckley's life—like any other life—has taken unexpected twists and turns. There have been changes in location, changes in roles, changes in daily routines. But each change has brought opportunities to rely on and nourish her ever-growing faith in the Savior and testimony of His restored church. As she has said:

During my lifetime it has been my great opportunity to see with my own eyes the fulfillment of prophecy as the Church has spread over the world. This is a new day, and a marvelous work and a wonder it is. My eyes fell upon these beautiful words of Nephi as he described his vision:

"It came to pass that I, Nephi, beheld the power of the Lamb of God, that it descended upon the saints of the church of the Lamb, and upon the covenant people of the Lord, who were scattered upon all the face of the earth; and they were armed with righteousness and with the power of God in great glory" (1 Nephi 14:14).

I have seen the power of great glory settle upon these covenant people who are scattered over the earth.

I have seen the power descend upon a Chinese woman who runs a prosperous export and import business with offices in the East Asia Bank Building on the island of Hong Kong.

She said: "You should have seen me when the elders found me. I was a chain smoker, pushing food over a counter where they came to eat. They told me they had a new religion they would like to tell me about. I laughed in their faces."

When I met this woman some five years after her baptism, I saw someone who did everything with an eye single to the glory of God. She had three beautiful children whom she was raising in the Church with only one desire in her heart—that they remain faithful.

Sometimes I just like to look out my window at the spires of the temple and the angel Moroni standing there steadfast and immovable. It makes everything in the world beautiful.

I love the Lord.

I know this is His work and that He is at the helm.

I have seen too much to ever deny it.

CHAPTER TWO

GENUINENESS

*

"I COULDN'T THINK OF ANYONE ELSE TO BE"

Marjorie, about 1914

37

Maybe it is because Marjorie Hinckley so clearly understands who she really is that she wastes very little energy in pretending, protecting, or defending herself. She immediately opens her circle and pulls you into her good world—whether you are one alone with her in conversation or one of ten thousand people in a foreign country listening to her translated remarks from a pulpit. Marjorie Hinckley possesses a heart without walls—she employs no artificial defenses to hide from others or shut them out. What you see is a good Christian woman, and that is what you get!

Evelyn P. Henriksen, a sister, relates a conversation that is representative of Sister Hinckley's charming genuineness:

At BYU a fireside was held in which Marjorie was featured with her daughters presenting incidents in her life. She had the audience of some twelve thousand in the palm of her hand. They chuckled throughout the evening at her refreshing sense of humor and jumped to their feet in a standing ovation at the conclusion. Later she expressed amazement at the response. My husband said, "Marge, they loved you because you were so relaxed and just yourself."

"I couldn't think of anyone else to be!" she quickly responded.

This genuineness immediately draws everyone in—through the front door and directly to the kitchen, without a pause in any formal parlors. Carolyn Rasmus, former administrative assistant to two Young Women general presidencies, recalls visiting Sister Hinckley and her three sisters one afternoon:

Usually I'm curious about how people decorate their homes: the furnishings, the pictures, the decorations, and the overall ambiance. But on an occasion when I had an opportunity to visit the home of President and Sister Hinckley, I never noticed these things. As I entered the door, I was greeted by the sounds of laughter and happy talk. Sister Hinckley, wearing her smocklike apron, motioned me to sit down and join with her and her three sisters. They likewise beckoned me warmly.

I immediately found myself included in a family conversation that was punctuated with laughter and fun. One sister had brought a humorous newspaper article about the "Olympic Event" we all enter when we drive in the reconstruction areas of the I-15 freeway. They had already read it, but wanted to share it with me. We all laughed heartily as we shared our own experiences driving this road. I felt as if I had always known these women. There was no pretense, no awkwardness in becoming acquainted. It seemed as though we were instant friends!

I asked about the gathering, and they told me how they get together once a week and what a wonderful time they have.

Immediately they began recalling conversations they'd recently had, ranging from experiences with e-mail to advice shared with daughters about a wide range of mother-daughter topics.

They reminisced about the times when their children were young and they would meet at their mother's home for similar gatherings. "Our children got to know each other well," one said, and they began remembering a different time and age, but one that reflected the same optimism and joy I sensed on that particular day. As I later related my experience to one of their children, she remembered those wonderful get-togethers. "I don't ever remember hearing them gossip or complain," she said. "Their conversation was always positive and happy. Wherever they were together, it was a happy, safe place to be."

No wonder I never noticed the pictures or the decor of the home. Everyone, including me, was having too much fun.

Patricia T. Holland comments on Sister Hinckley's down-to-earth style:

One gets the feeling around Sister Hinckley that she is absolutely unconcerned with the fads and fancies of the secular world. She is comfortable with kings and queens, princes and prime ministers, but she is just as comfortable—and probably more interested in—the newest member of the Church she just met in a distant land or the youngest child present in some far-flung congregation of the Saints she has just attended. You get the feeling that she sees right to the heart of everything and everyone. The idea that anyone could be false or pompous or self-aggrandizing with Marjorie Hinckley is

In Tabernacle for general conference

39

unimaginable. She has a radarlike sense of honesty, humility, genuineness, and sincerity.

To quote both Sister Frances Monson and Sister Ruth Faust, "She is a real lady!" There is something in that compliment from two of the women who know her best that speaks of the dignity and character that come from being absolutely genuine. In Sister Hinckley, what you see is what you get—and that is what everyone wants to get! Her love, her honest interest in you as a person, her lack of affectation and self-aggrandizement, her faith—she is the real thing, she is a real lady. Marjorie Hinckley fits perfectly the position the Lord has placed her in—standing side by side with our prophet, President Gordon B. Hinckley.

Sister Hinckley has often spoken about self-acceptance. Certainly an acceptance of herself undergirds her ability to be genuine.

I recently read a study of 275 college men and women. It revealed that over 90 percent suffered from gnawing, frustrated feelings of deficiency. They gave all sorts of reasons: physical incompetence, unpleasant appearance, lack of social charm, failure in love, low intellectual ability. To me a form of compensation is almost always possible. The homely young woman may develop the more wit and charm because she is homely. The shy youth with a temperament of a recluse may find a useful niche in scientific research.

No well-integrated life is possible without self-acceptance. If you are shy, accept it. If you have no musical ability, accept it, as though to say: "I, John Smith, hereby accept myself with my inherited endowments and the elements in my environment that I cannot control, and I will now see what I can do with this John Smith."

One of the ablest women in this country, now the wife of a university president, was brought up in poverty. She recalls an occasion when, as a girl, she complained of her hardships to her mother. "See here," said the mother. "I have given you life. That is probably all I will ever be able to give you. Now you stop complaining and do something with it."

A favorite quote from Sister Hinckley's files describes her contentment with what she is—and what she is not:

"Find out what you love to do, what you can do best, and do it. Each man has his own special powers, each man can do at least one thing a little better than millions of other men.

"All about us, we see dissatisfaction—people wishing they were someone else, had someone else's abilities" (Sydney J. Harris).

Sister Hinckley gives simple language to this very hopeful way of evaluating our own performance:

We each do the best we can. My best may not be as good as your best, but it's my best. The fact is that we know when we are doing our best and when we are not. If we are not doing our best, it leaves us with a gnawing hunger and frustration. But when we do our level best, we experience a peace.

She recalls an example of doing her best and finding peace:

I was once asked to speak to a Relief Society on the role of women. I had just read the talk that Pat Holland had given at a BYU Women's Conference and that was published in the July 1980 *Ensign*. I loved it. It was scholarly.

Marjorie in 1933

It was perceptive. It was, in my mind, a small masterpiece. I read it through three times. This was the kind of talk I wanted to give.

I sat down at the typewriter and rolled in a clean sheet of white paper. And then I sat there. Nothing happened. After several minutes staring at the blank paper I realized that I was no Pat Holland. Try as I would, I could never write that kind of a talk. I left the typewriter for an hour or so, until the cobwebs cleared from my brain and I could accept the fact that the only kind of talk I could write would have to be the one that could come out of the mind of Marge Hinckley. It would be no Pat Holland masterpiece, but it would be my best effort. I remembered the words in D&C 46:11–12:

"For all have not every gift given unto them; for there are many gifts, and to every man [and woman] is given a gift by the Spirit of God. To some is given one, and to some is given another, that all may be profited thereby."

I was at peace.

A conversation between Sister Hinckley and one of her daughters is a lighthearted expression of her confidence in who she is—and who she is not:

Mother was getting ready for an occasion when I dropped by the apartment late one afternoon. When she told me where she was going—as she reached for a pleated skirt and white cotton blouse—I gasped. "Mother, this is a huge thing," I protested. "The reception is in honor of Dad and you. He's probably going to wear a tux. Every woman there will have on sequins and diamonds."

Continuing to dress, completely unruffled, she said, "Well, I don't have any sequins in my closet. But this skirt is black, and the blouse does have a lace collar. And besides that, if we're the guests of honor, whatever I wear will have to be right!"

Two granddaughters share their feelings about their grandmother's easy-going attitude toward life:

Grandma never competes. She's happy with who she is and who you are. Everyone is a winner, except when it comes to sports. Then BYU must win!

*****

One thing I love about my Grandma is her honesty. I remember being at a play once with Grandpa and Grandma—she would often take us to Christmas plays—and a man came up to my grandpa and said, "Hi, President Hinckley. Do you remember me? I met you twenty years ago at a stake conference in . . ." My grandma leaned over to me and said, "I just don't understand how he remembers people after all these years. At least he's polite and always tries. When people ask me if I remember them after meeting them so long ago, I simply say, 'No. I'm sorry, I don't remember you. What is your name?'" I had to laugh at that.

Duane Cardall, a television reporter in Salt Lake City, Utah, has accompanied the Hinckleys on several of their tours throughout the Church. He fondly recalls his experiences:

Whether at home or in remote regions of the world, the Latter-day Saints flock to see and honor their prophet, seer, and revelator, and then they fall in love with his wife. They're immediately attracted to this diminutive woman with the grandmotherly demeanor and the cherubic smile. It was my pleasure to observe her in meeting after meeting as she accompanied her husband to Great Britain on his first international visit after becoming president of the Church.

It's obvious that the few who are privileged to actually meet and interact with Sister Hinckley immediately feel comfortable in her presence. Unfortunately, the demands on the president's time as well as concerns for the couple's health and safety preclude many one-on-one encounters. But even those who see her only at the pulpit and hear her comments from a distance experience her genuineness and especially her disarming humor.

Opening her remarks in one of the meetings, she told a British audience: "On our way to England once a few years ago we stopped in Detroit to see some of our grandchildren, and our little three-year-old granddaughter cried to come with me. Her mother said, 'You can't go with Grandma. She's going to London.' And this little three-year-old said, 'But London is my favorite town.' She wasn't very brainwashed!"

In that instant, she had her British audience in the palm of her hand, and they sat waiting for her message. That's her style—make them laugh and feel good, and then proceed to leave a message filled with practical advice. During my travels with the Hinckleys, I must admit, I've looked forward to hearing her brief sermons as much as her husband's.

Wherever she goes, whatever the audience, she comes across with disarming genuineness and sincerity.

Ardeth Kapp, former Young Women General President, shares similar feelings:

"Sister Hinckley is so real" is the description often used in describing her influence in people's lives. She is not one who would want to be held up as a perfect model to intimidate others. Rather, she is one of our beloved sisters to walk beside, learn from, laugh with, and follow, knowing that she understands and cares.

On a spring evening in 1996, the Marriott Center on the BYU campus was filled almost to capacity for a BYU Women's Conference fireside: "An Evening with Marjorie Hinckley and Daughters." Thousands of sisters were for a brief time drawn into the Hinckley family circle. I was seated on the fifth row from the front, a little to the side of the platform where Sister Hinckley was seated at a table with her daughters on both sides of her.

The large audience quieted as the strains of organ music filled the Marriott Center. We had no way of knowing for sure what to expect, but the presenters on the platform became the focus of everyone's attention. It appeared that each of the four had a copy of the script they intended to follow. The presentation was going smoothly, a warm and delightful conversation between mother and daughters. Suddenly there was a brief hesitation, a pause, and then Sister Hinckley began chuckling and shifting the papers in front of her as she spoke. The microphones were well placed; we all heard. "I've lost my place," she said. "Where are we?" Her daughter Virginia, now joining the chuckling, gave immediate assistance, and the dialogue continued. There was no sense of embarrassment.

A little later, the formal preparation once again seemed to be a hindrance, and it appeared from where I was sitting that Sister Hinckley set aside the script. She laughingly gave up the formality of speaking to an "audience" and just began visiting with each of us one by one. She was so open, so honest, so real and unassuming—there was nothing to hide and no pretense. She spoke with humor and warmth and gratitude as she told of earlier days in her marriage and some of the challenges she had experienced.

The conversation at one point was focused on the period of the Great Depression. In a teasing way, Sister Hinckley and her daughters told of how President Hinckley typically referred to any time around those years as "the bottom of the Depression." At this point a video clip appeared on the large overhead screen. Even if the discarded script had been followed exactly, the timing could not have been better. The lights went down, and the tape was beginning to roll. There was President Hinckley on the screen ready to make his contribution reflecting on memories of the past. In a warm but serious tone, he began, "It was in the bottom of the Depression . . ." Sister Hinckley, her daughters, and the entire audience erupted into laughter. It was as if we had all been included in this fun family banter.

On this occasion, President Hinckley was sitting not on the stand but in the audience on the front row, where he was able to observe his family. I was sitting just a few seats behind him, a little to the side, where I could easily observe his responses during the meeting. At this point he became the center of attention for those of us who could see him. He immediately broke into laughter. He laughed and laughed, his shoulders shaking as he became the center of the fun. It was a wonderful invitation for the audience to be able to join in the teasing.

However, the best was yet to come. When the family's final words of wisdom, encouragement, faith, and inspiration had been

With daughters at 1996 BYU/Relief Society Women's Conference fireside

spoken, it was as though President Hinckley could restrain himself no longer. He left his seat on the front row and walked up the few steps to the podium. All eyes were on him as we waited and watched, wondering what the prophet would have to say to us on this occasion when we had been privileged to come a little closer to him and his family.

He didn't have anything to say to us—not in words, that is. At this moment it was not the crowd that had brought President Hinckley to his feet. With a hand on his wife's shoulder, he leaned over and tenderly gave her a kiss, and then gave the same token of love to each of his daughters. He then stepped to the back of the platform, away from center stage.

The scriptural statement "Neither is the man without the woman, neither the woman without the man, in the Lord" (1 Corinthians 11:11) was exemplified in this brief and tender exchange. As their separate positions of prominence were reversed on this occasion—she in the spotlight and he in the supporting role—it was evident to all that President Hinckley was a loving, tender husband and father, and that Sister Hinckley was a woman of great stature at the center of her family circle. We were taken in by the honesty and genuineness of it all.

Barbara Ballard, wife of Elder M. Russell Ballard of the Twelve, offers another concurring voice:

The sparkle that emanates from the countenance of Sister Marjorie Hinckley is contagious and captures the heart of everyone. She is truly "one of us," meaning the women of the Church. She never considers her position as being above anyone. I have heard her say on several occasions, "I sometimes feel I need to pinch myself to help me realize I'm actually here and associating with all these wonderful people." I don't believe she will ever get over the wonder of it.

Mary Ellen Edmunds, former director of training at the Missionary Training Center in Provo, Utah, has warm memories of Sister Hinckley's humor and genuineness:

I was serving in the Southern Far East Mission in 1963 and had been transferred from the mission office in Hong Kong to the Philippines, one of the three zones in our mission. Shortly after the transfer, we learned that our mission president had been in a very serious accident in Hong Kong and was in the hospital. We didn't see him for seven months, and we were many miles away in another country.

One of the ways in which we were helped was to receive some additional visits from the General Authority who was our supervisor in Asia, Elder Gordon B. Hinckley. How we loved and enjoyed him!

With no thought that it might be inappropriate to write to a General Authority, I wrote some letters to him and his family. One time I had what I thought was a very clever idea. We had an abundance of tiny little bugs in the Philippines—ants, fleas, bedbugs, termites, mosquitoes, flies, and baby cockroaches. I got some clear tape and stuck a variety of these little critters onto pieces of paper to make what I thought was a very unusual, attractive letterhead. I began sending these letters to everyone, knowing they'd be cherished.

One of these pieces of homemade stationery was sent to Elder and Sister Hinckley far away in Utah. The next time Sister Hinckley came with her husband to the Philippines, she had a surprise for me.

In Hong Kong we often had a treat called Smarties, small candies that came in a cardboard tube about the size of a pencil. When Sister Hinckley arrived, she gave me one of these "Smartie tubes" with a happy smile. Inside the tube I found a lively little bug-eating lizard—a gecko!

Somehow I realized that Sister Hinckley wanted to help us cut down on the bug and critter population in our little apartment in the Philippines. (Maybe she was also saying that one of those "critter letters" was enough.)

I've loved her ever since. She was REAL! And to her, *we* were real, too.

There is a tremendous warmth in a mother who isn't trying to be someone else, as one daughter attests:

When we were young, it was very uncommon to have mothers in the classroom—or anywhere at school. I remember only one day. We were having a program in the lunchroom. Chairs lined the room, and the children sat in them as we waited for the mothers to arrive. I noticed with curious interest as each mother came in and then made her way to sit with her child. The mother who came through the door just before mine was wearing spiked heels and a darling dress and had all of this foofy hair. Yes, she was young and, I thought, beautiful. In fact, she looked like a teenager. As she made her way over to her tap-dancer daughter (of course, I thought), I looked up to see my mother come through the same door. With that instant juxtaposition, I will never forget the flood of security and happiness I felt when I saw her—no foofy hair or spiked heels, not very young or very beautiful, dressed in her typically tidy house-dress. There was a warm, comfortable feeling and the thought clear as neon: "Oh, I'm so glad that my mother looks like a real mother! Whatever would a person do if her only mother wore darling dresses and had painted fingernails?"

Margaret Smoot, a freelance writer and producer and former spokesperson for Brigham Young University, sums up the down-to-earth attitude that characterizes this very real woman:

Like most members of the Church, I have not had extended time in Sister Hinckley's presence. My contact with her has been primarily electronic. I have watched her on television news as she and her husband have undertaken their many marathon, whirlwind presidential travels. I have had glimpses of her on historic visits to China, traversing the gentle landscape of England, greeting Saints in South America, and shaking hands and waving to throngs of well-wishers closer to home. There she is, unfailingly good-spirited, gracious, walking briskly side by side with her husband.

And usually she is wearing her sensible shoes, chosen for comfort above all other factors. If I knew nothing else of Sister Hinckley, that alone would be testimony of her values and priorities. Sister Hinckley does not do things to impress. She does them for the right reason—because they make sense to her and to the Lord. If you are going to keep up with President Gordon B. Hinckley, she seems to be saying, you must really wear track shoes, with good soles. And keep up she does.

With a prophet known for his quick wit, his wife is his mirror image on matters of humor. Marjorie Hinckley keeps up easily with her husband on that score. And who is to say that she doesn't often best him, quip for quip?

But besting him is not on the agenda for Sister Hinckley. Nor is keeping score. She is a remarkable and exemplary woman who has found a receptive spot in the hearts of Latter-day Saints for the buoyancy she brings to her duties—accompanying her husband in his official capacity as prophet, seer, and revelator of the restored Church of Jesus Christ.

We can't know all their specific challenges, but we can appreciate how high the expectations are and how well they are doing what is asked of them. We can't walk in Sister Hinckley's sensible shoes, but we can emulate her stride. We can learn from her strength and character and down-to-earth qualities, knowing that we will all take a turn in and out of the spotlight, and that, like Sister Hinckley, we too must keep our priorities straight and our identity intact when the multitudes are not present.

Marjorie with grandmother, mother, and aunt

CHAPTER THREE

MOTHERING

*

"HAVE JOY IN YOUR CHILDREN"

In a Mother's Day sacrament meeting speech, Sister Hinckley aptly expressed her own happiness in being a mother:

Jewish women have a wonderful way of bidding each other good-bye. They say, "Have joy in your children."

And so I say to you, "Have joy in your mothering," whether you are the mother, the aunt, the grandmother, the next-door neighbor. We all have the opportunity to be an influence for good.

Sheri Dew, in her biography of President Hinckley, wrote of how his wife looked forward to summers when her children were young:

[She] loved the sound of the screen door slamming shut as children ran in from the backyard. . . . Marjorie savored the days she had her five to herself, and she went to great lengths to keep summers unstructured so her young ones would have time to lie in the gully and listen to the birds sing if they wanted to. She wept each fall when it was time to send her brood back to school; even when school was in session she looked forward to the moment each day when her children burst through the door and started scrounging for an afternoon snack. One day when Dick had to stay after school for some grade-school discipline, Marjorie marched over to his classroom and announced to his startled teacher, "You can do anything you want with this boy all day long, but after 3 P.M. *he's mine.*"

Sister Hinckley offers some insights on effective mothering:

Children rise higher when they are treated with respect. Use courteous and respectful language when you talk with one another. We have always had pretty clear expectations in our home about using respectful language. One day our little granddaughter had been playing with a friend and came home quite upset about something the friend had said. Her mother asked her what it was. She responded, "Well, it's such a bad word that I can't say it, but it was "shut [point upward]!"

A world-famous child psychologist, Bruno Bettelheim, said at the age of eighty-four, "You can't teach children to be good. The best you can do for your child is to live a good life yourself. What a parent knows and believes, the child will lean on."

You don't teach a child not to hit by hitting. We cannot expect to be respected if we treat others in demeaning ways.

*****

Our children grew up in a semi-rural area. We had a fairly

large piece of property with lawns and gardens and orchards and plenty of work to keep the boys out of mischief. A wooded ravine ran through the property; we called it "the hollow."

One day our oldest boy turned up missing. There were lawns to be mowed, irrigation ditches to be cleaned. The hours ticked away. All afternoon I practiced a speech I would give him when he showed up. And show up he did, at mealtime, which I knew he would. "Where have you been?" I asked.

"Down in the hollow."

"And what have you been doing down in the hollow?"

His reply, "Nothing."

Some years later I had reason to be glad that I had not given him the speech. He was home from his mission and a senior at the university. It was test week. He was under a lot of pressure to do well in order to get into the graduate school of his choice. Things were not going too well with his girlfriend. The pressures of adult life were beginning to be felt. I watched him as he drove home from school one afternoon. He got out of the car, kicked a clod of dirt, went over to examine the swelling buds on the lilac tree, came in the kitchen, straddled a chair backwards, and said, "Mom, I had a wonderful childhood, didn't I?"

"Well, I hope so. You did your share of complaining about all the work that had to be done."

"Oh, it was wonderful," he said. "Those long summer days, when you could lie on your back in the hollow and listen to the birds sing and watch the ants build their castles."

The memory of the peace of a summer day—"God's in his heaven, and all's right with the world"—sustained him when the pressures of adult life began to crowd in.

Things are different now. Children hear so many voices from

so many directions. There are so few empty summer days. There are pressures to excel. It has become a challenge to let children be children.

It has never been so important that children have a home that is a place of refuge, a place of peace, a place of unconditional love—even when the report card may not be what you hoped for.

*****

My mother taught me some basic philosophies of rearing children. One is that you have to trust children. I tried hard never to say "no" if I could possibly say "yes." I think that worked well because it gave my children the feeling that I trusted them and they were responsible to do the best they could.

Kathleen H. Hinckley, a daughter-in-law, writes:

In my early years of motherhood, I would call my mother-in-law any time I needed some advice about the dilemmas of child rearing. She would listen with compassion and without criticism. Even though I was thousands of miles away, she could relate exactly.

I remember a time when my oldest daughter wanted to come to Salt Lake to spend some time with her cousin. The arrangements couldn't be worked out, and my daughter cried herself to sleep. I could taste the tears and feel the choking sobs in my own throat. I called Grandma for advice, wondering if we should go to greater lengths to work out the trip. Grandma's comforting words were, "She will be all right. She'll learn that that's life, and she'll learn that she can accept disappointment and get over it."

Marjorie (front row, second from right) at birthday party

55

Another time the concern was about swimming lessons. All the mothers were tossing their reluctant, screaming children into the teacher's outstretched arms in the pool. I just could not bring myself to do the same, but I did want our son to learn to swim. When I called her for advice, she verbalized something I would say over and over to myself for many years to come, "Just save the relationship." I believe those words are the most simple and powerful parenting principle I have ever learned. Long before she verbalized this principle to me, I had seen her as a living example of it.

I first became acquainted with the Hinckley family in Boston. Clark, to whom I was about to become engaged, was graduating from business school in a few weeks, and several members of the family gathered in Boston to attend his graduation on June 12, 1973.

One hot, muggy day I was with the extended family on the subway speeding toward downtown Boston from Cambridge when we realized that Clark's two-year-old nephew had stripped to his diapers. Without missing a beat in the conversation, Grandma dressed him. Before anyone knew it, he had taken his clothes off. She put them on and then they were off again! Giggling, Clark's mother said, "It's just too hot for clothes," and the happy two-year-old spent the day sightseeing in diapers. It was my first introduction to the Hinckley way of allowing each family member, whenever possible, to be himself. I was being taught that even two-year-olds have feelings that are important and respected.

A couple of years later, that same little boy did not have any desire to be in the family photograph. Every encouraging antic was performed in hopes of enticing the reluctant child to line up with the family. After all, we were all gathered in Salt Lake from all over the world—Hawaii to New York—and no one knew when we would be together again for such an opportunity. However, I remember the amazement I felt when the prevailing attitude in Grandma's living room that afternoon was that it was no big deal. Nobody got really tense, and sooner or later—I don't remember exactly how—the picture was taken and we were all in it.

In the meantime, all of the relationships were saved.

Sister Hinckley's sons both recall another of her parenting techniques:

President Benson counseled mothers, "Praise your children more than you correct them. Praise them for even their smallest achievement." Mother was an expert at this principle, even when there appeared to be very little to praise! She believed we could do anything we set our minds to do, so if we didn't perform well, she assumed either the situation was unfair or we had simply failed to apply ourselves!

*****

Some of my earliest recollections of Mother revolve around our year or so in Denver. I was three turning four years of age. I had contracted rheumatic fever, and it fell to Mother to take me to the hospital for regular tests, including the dreaded EKG or electrocardiogram. I say "dreaded" not because it was painful but because the terrible anticipation of a negative outcome, which would indicate that the disease had spread to my heart, could be read in Mother's face.

Even at four years of age I was quite a handful. Most mothers would have been a little devious, using a ploy like this: "Let's go for ice cream," and then, once inside the car, completing the sentence with, "after our visit to the hospital."

Mother, unable to tell even the whitest of lies, would simply tell me to get in the car, it was time for a visit to the hospital. I would sit on the living-room floor and kick up a fuss that could be heard around the neighborhood. Finally, she would take my arm and literally drag me to the car and put me in the backseat, and off we would go, with me convinced she was the meanest, most heartless thing on the planet. I didn't realize for years that the hollow-sounding, "This hurts me more than it is going to hurt you," was true. It made her miserable to see me so sick and frightened.

Once strapped into the EKG rig, I was told to hold as still as a mouse so the machine could do its work. This I did superbly for a four-year-old, and I could hardly wait to get home so that I could hurry next door. I would strut into my friend Kay's house and say, "I'll bet you can't hold as still as I can. Watch this!" And I would go into a freeze for about a minute. Sure enough, I won the hold-still contest every time. No one even came close.

You see, Mother had praised me so much for how well I submitted to the EKG tests, including holding as still as a mouse, that I was convinced there was something adulatory about that particular talent. Mom seemed to get a big kick out of these demonstrations to Kay and to the rest of my family, and she would say, "That's right, Dick held as still as a mouse!" The happy ending to that story is that after several weeks in bed, with her tending to my needs, after many trips to the hospital, the rheumatic fever left without ever affecting my heart. When the doctor told us the good news, I couldn't understand why Mother cried.

Sister Hinckley has spoken convincingly to young people about home and the need for love:

With Kathleen and Richard, around 1943

58

Honor thy father and thy mother is one of the Ten Commandments and probably one of the most challenging of all the principles of the gospel for our young people. From my own experience let me tell you that the day is not far off when you will be the mother or the father and someone whom you have not yet seen will be the daughter or the son.

The trouble with the world and the trouble with you and me is that we don't love each other enough. And if we do, we don't bother to show it, or we don't bother to say it. If the world is to know love, it has to begin at home. It has to be in your heart and in mine. And the place to begin is home. I have been shaken and saddened lately by some instances where there has been estrangement between parents and children.

Did you ever stop to think what a terrible responsibility you are to your parents? Not only are they required to feed you and clothe you and educate you, but from the moment you were placed in their keeping it became their responsibility to see that you are taught to live a life that is fitting for a child of God, that you might someday return to Him as pure as the day you came. What a staggering responsibility! We feel it. Most of the mistakes we make are because we love you so much. We are so anxious for you to do your best that we get clumsy in our anxiety. We don't know how to communicate with you and we bungle. But it is only because we love you. And you had better appreciate it, because no one will ever love you as much. Your husband will love you, your wife will love you, but let me disillusion you right now—it will not be the way your mother and father love you. Theirs is as close to an unselfish love as we know on this earth.

Being a son or a daughter is probably the hardest role you

have to play. Home is where you are loved the most and act the worst. But I have come to the conclusion that it is in the home where we are tested the most. Most of us have developed a pretty good set of company manners that we exercise at school and socials and church and other places, but it is what we are at home that tells the true story of what we really are. The family unit is fundamental. I wonder if this was so there would be some area where we would function with our guard down so that the Lord could see what we really are.

If you are looking for a good husband or a good wife, find out how your friend treats his parents and his brothers and sisters. Then you will know pretty much how he is going to treat his wife and children. If a girl is rude to her mother—if she talks to her in a loud and sassy voice, if she ignores her counsel and argues with her and says cutting things to her—beware. If she behaves this way in the privacy of her parents' home, she most likely will behave the same in the privacy of her own home. Think of yourself, too. Unless you can learn to live with your parents in love and kindness and respect and helpfulness, pity the person who marries you.

The family is eternal. Love must be nurtured. We must put our pride and our haughtiness and our misunderstandings away and say, "I love you, Mother. I love you, Father. What would you have me do?" You can never be happy under any other circumstances.

On another occasion, she addressed a few remarks to young mothers in a Mother's Day sacrament meeting:

As I watched some of the young mothers come into this

meeting with young children, restless from meetings that have preceded this one, I think I felt something of your frustration and challenge to be the perfect mother. Relax. There is no such thing as the perfect mother who fits all the eulogies. We just do the best we can with the help of the Lord, and who knows, these children who are struggling to be free may someday rise up and call us blessed.

The trick is to enjoy it. Don't wish away your days of caring for young children. This is your great day. Sometimes we get so caught up in the physical work and trivia that we forget the big picture. We forget whose children they really are. When the house is filled with children, noise and teasing and laughter, you get the feeling this is forever. Before you know it they will be gone. When our second son went away to school at the age of seventeen, I said, "But Clark, I am not through with you. I feel there is so much I will need to teach you."

"Too late, Mother, too late."

Our children grow so quickly out of our reach.

The rewards of mothering are not immediate. There are times when you are less than appreciated. I took from the oven one day what I thought was a beautiful casserole, only to have my six-year-old son say, "Mom, how come you baked the garbage?"

Then there is the unexpected hug, when you least deserve it. And while you are enjoying these days of mothering, be sure

Marjorie with children on family vacation

61

your demands on your children for perfection are not so heavy that they cannot be children.

Don't be like the mother I know who said to her ten-year-old daughter, who was the oldest of five children and from whom the mother needed a little help and cooperation, "Sometimes you act just like a child."

"But Mother, I am," she wisely replied.

A busy parent writes: "One morning I was hurrying my three-year-old's dressing procedure because I had only minutes to spare. In the middle of the commotion and worry, my little girl cleverly enjoyed a little joke of her own about something unrelated to the job at hand. I ignored her fun and indicated my disapproval. . . . Her sweet, thought-provoking response: 'Mommy, don't we even have time to laugh?'"

We all feel the pressures and stress of the sophisticated, fast-paced, complicated, competitive world in which we find ourselves. Not only do we feel it as adults, but the children feel it too. Because of TV, the press, and videos, our children are exposed to adult life very, very early. This makes it doubly important that mothers and fathers consciously strive to make it possible for children to be children before they become adults.

Marjorie Hinckley was a stay-at-home mother in the days when that was the rule rather than the exception. In a very real way she was at the center of family life—usually in the kitchen—for the entire day. Gardening, canning, cleaning, painting, bathing babies, feeding, changing diapers, sorting, cooking, washing, organizing, beautifying, sewing, hugging, listening. That's what she did.

And so in 1955, when she was invited to travel with her husband to prepare for the dedication of the Swiss Temple, it was a big change in routine for Marjorie and the children. The oldest of the five was sixteen, the youngest eighteen months. The absence was to be for six weeks. This may sound like a recipe for disaster, but with her exceptional ability to "mother" even across an ocean, it remains one of the times the grown children like to remember. Her uncanny gifts of nurturing, building, including, and loving came through loud and clear in letters. One of the boys remembers:

Those of us who were old enough to read and remember will never forget her letters. They started to arrive about ten days after our parents had left, and it seems we got either a letter or a series of postcards every day thereafter. They even kept coming for a few days after they returned. Mother told us about the preparations being made for the dedication, the people who were working on the grounds, the flood in the basement, the crisis in the laundry. I will never forget the visual image those letters created in my mind of a land where everything was spotlessly clean, where green grass and flowers grew to the very edge of the roads, where beautiful little chalets lined country roads, and where snow-covered Alps towered majestically above sky-blue lakes and streams. The letters transfixed us, not just with her childlike awe, which was palpable, or with her lifelike descriptions of places and people, but also with her expressions of fondness for us.

Oh, how she missed us, and how proud she was of us! She was the luckiest person in the world, she would write, not just to be experiencing that beautiful country with Dad but because she had such wonderful children at home whom she could hardly wait to see, and in whom she had complete faith and trust. Little did she know that our baby-sitter was not quite as fond of us as our mother was, and we had "given her the weekends off"—which she gladly took! There is much more to that story, but it does not reflect credit on Mother, rather discredit on her offspring.

Marjorie Hinckley's joy in mothering is undergirded by her humility and meekness. Her son Richard remembers this trait in a story he calls "Mothering with Meekness":

Mother was not a strict disciplinarian, nor was she a hard taskmaster. There was plenty of work to do, but she was never very good at getting mad if we approached our tasks with indolence, or even ignored her repeated requests to complete this chore or that. And Mother never swore. And I mean *never!* Except once.

Kathy and her friend Bobbie Olson were playing at our house. They were about twelve years old. It was a summer day, and they were in and out of the house, racing around acting their age. Mom was trying to tell them something, and they ignored her and were probably a little sassy. They were getting on her nerves, and I remember watching her frustration mount. They were being, in a word, naughty.

Getting nowhere and totally exasperated, Mother finally blurted out, "Damn you girls!" Well, the world might as well have stopped! I was shocked. Kathy was shocked. Bobbie was shocked. Most of all, Mother was shocked. She froze in her tracks, covered her mouth with her hand, and said incredulously, "Oh dear, did I say that?"

Instead of staying mad at the girls, she said, "Oh, I am so sorry I said that. Can you girls ever forgive me? I think I had better go and wash my mouth out with soap!" And she did! That was our punishment if ever we said anything we should not have said, and she wanted to make sure we saw her do the same.

Then she went to her bedroom and sat on the edge of her bed

and cried. I felt terrible. Kathy and Bobbie felt terrible. I never heard her swear again.

As Sister Hinckley's children grew and married, she opened her arms to sons-in-law and daughters-in-law with the same acceptance and love she gave her own children. A son-in-law, Jim Pearce, remembers:

Becoming a member of the Hinckley family is not an undertaking that one approaches lightly. It is intimidating. You are facing a father-in-law who is constantly in the company of the brightest and the best and who treasures his daughters and wants the best for them. Could he settle for less? Could he settle for me? Yet, when his daughter and my future wife fell in love with me, I could not pass up the opportunity to give my children such a mother and to enjoy life with such a companion. I went forward with trepidation.

This is where Sister Hinckley came into my life. No one could love a mother-in-law more than I love her. She has always—from my first meeting with her—been completely accepting of me and shown great love. She has always made me feel most welcome, always been supportive and shown great faith in me as I have faced various life choices. She has never been critical. Her happy ways are a delight to be around.

She seemed to believe in me as much as my own mother did, and in my potential to provide a secure, stable, and happy home for her daughter and her grandchildren. That degree of love, trust, and confidence keeps me forever duty-bound to be a better and nobler person than I might otherwise have been.

In the movie *Gone with the Wind*, Rhett Butler says of Melanie at the time of her death, "She was the only completely kind person I ever knew. A great lady. A very great lady." When I hear those words I always think of my mother-in-law, Marjorie Hinckley.

Kathleen H. Hinckley expresses similar sentiments:

She has been the greatest mother-in-law anyone could ever imagine. She has treated me like one of hers from the very beginning. One of my treasured pieces of jewelry is a beautiful pearl bracelet from her travels to Hong Kong. She gave it to me the first time she came to visit us in New York after Clark and I were married. She told me she had given one to all her daughters many years ago and she had saved this one in anticipation of Clark finding me. "I'm glad he finally did," she concluded.

She has always remembered my birthday with a card expressing her confidence in and her love for me. Often a gift arrived in the mail with some money and a note with strict instructions to buy something I would not otherwise buy for myself.

Sister Hinckley continues to mother her adult children in ways that not only build them but enhance their relationships with one another, as her daughter Virginia describes:

When we lived away from Salt Lake we looked forward to visits from Dad and Mother as they went to and fro on Church assignments. The usual pattern was (if we were on the flight path) to arrange the itinerary to stop in or near our city. Either Dad would stay over one night, taking a flight to Salt Lake in the morning, or we would just take the children and visit at the airport between connecting flights. But Mother would usually stay for a couple of days. You could always count on a boost. She must have been tired, but the conversation never got to that. She would crawl into bed with a child while I put a baby down for the night. I could hear her telling wide-eyed little girls about South Africa, ostrich eggs, azaleas, and the temple that had just been dedicated—and how their grandpa's talks were the very best of all the talks in all the dedicatory sessions!

She'd clean an oven, defrost a refrigerator, shine your kitchen windows, all the while chatting about how wonderful your children were, what a good father your husband was, what nice friends there were in your neighborhood, and what an amazing job you were doing. She was the lifeline between all the members of the family— she told you what was happening at Clark's house, where she'd been a few weeks before. How precociously funny his children were, how gracious and amazing his wife was. About Alan's new job, Kathy's church calling. Jane's new boyfriend. Dick and Jane's new baby. That Dad was proudly telling someone the other day about you and your family. We got those messages through Mother—unabashed, face-to-face praise was never Dad's style.

She was our connector during the early busy family years when we didn't have enough time to write frequent letters or enough money to call long distance. She'd listen to us worry about this child and that, and somehow after we had explained all our frustrations and fears, they were gone. We knew that she'd go home and keep thinking about it for us! And sometimes there'd be a reassuring call or a letter days later: "I've been thinking about _____. You know, I don't think it's a problem. She's going to be okay."

Sister Hinckley's mothering extended beyond her immediate family. A nephew, Scott Wadsworth, shares an experience:

On August 20, 1957, at the age of nine, I had the misfortune of breaking my wrist while playing on the chicken coop in the back corner of our large lot in the little town of Panaca, Nevada.

Mother and Aunt Bea drove me to the hospital in nearby Caliente. The doctor, recognizing a compound fracture that he couldn't treat, gave me something for the pain, and as soon as Dad got home we were off to Salt Lake City to the LDS Hospital.

After surgery and six days in the hospital, my mother, President Hinckley's youngest sister, arranged for me to stay at Aunt Marge and Uncle Gord's house so that she and Dad could go home to care for their other nine children.

Looking back, I am sure that Aunt Marge did many things during this period that would not have normally been on her busy schedule. She was unselfishly kind and caring and made me feel like part of the family. She helped me to cope with homesickness and took me to many doctor appointments. I remember that after each doctor visit, she would take me and whichever of her children were with us to Snelgrove's for ice cream.

At the end of two weeks, while I was visiting the doctor, without warning to either Aunt Marge or myself he rebroke my arm like you would a piece of firewood. It was terribly painful. That night Aunt Marge kept a constant vigil over me as though I were her own son. The next morning she was the one to take me back to the LDS Hospital for another surgery. And then back to her home to recover again.

Over that several-week period, I learned to love the Hinckley family, especially sweet Aunt Marge, who had become my second mother.

Russell Osguthorpe, who grew up next door to the Hinckleys, also saw Sister Hinckley as a second mother:

For the first nine years of my life the Hinckleys were my next-door neighbors. When my family moved a few miles away, the Hinckleys still seemed like neighbors because I spent so much time with their son Clark. Their home was a place where any child would have felt safe, a place where everyone was accepted, a place where creativity and initiative were encouraged. When Clark and I wanted to make some money selling Kool-Aid, increase our collection of discarded license plates, or fly a kite in the field that adjoined the Hinckleys' property, Sister Hinckley would always give us the help we requested. If we needed a ride, she would go immediately in search of a pillow for the car seat—she was too short to see over the steering wheel—and her glasses. Neither of these was ever easy to find.

When it came time to plan the program for my missionary farewell, I asked Sister Hinckley if she would be the featured speaker. With a smile, she unhesitatingly responded, "Gordon would be happy to speak at your farewell." With a little more resolve, I responded, "But I'm asking you to speak." She told me that she would think about it, but that her husband would be the better choice. The next day she agreed to speak at my farewell.

She began her talk on that Sunday evening in 1966 with a smile in her voice as she said: "Russell has been in our home so much with our children that sometimes as I've been tossing the orders and chastisements about, I've had to remind myself that I was not his mother."

She went on to describe the kind of relationships that developed among children and parents in our neighborhood: "For something like fifteen years the Osguthorpes' kitchen door and our kitchen door were separated by a driveway and a huge box elder tree. These were wonderful years, and years that are becoming more precious to us as time passes. There were summer nights filled with children playing Run, Sheepy, Run and Kick the Can. There were green apples, bee stings, and secret hiding places in the hollow. There were vegetable gardens whose peas never reached the kitchen and irrigation water that had to be held back or coaxed forward. But most of all, in that neighborhood, there was love. And it was a love we didn't have to talk about; it was just there."

As I reflect on those days, I am convinced that Sister Hinckley was one of the primary reasons we experienced the love she described. She would never have taken any credit for it. She just saw herself doing what the Lord had called her to do: be a good wife and mother. But in the process of carrying out what some see as menial tasks of parenthood, Sister Hinckley nurtured more than her own children.

Kathy Bagley Garff, another neighbor, remembers a precious—if difficult—learning experience:

When I was a young girl I remember sleeping out in the backyard regularly with the neighbor kids. One morning very early, we all decided to help ourselves to Obert and Grace Tanner's cherries, just waiting to be picked and enjoyed. We quietly climbed the tree and overindulged ourselves. After all, there were plenty of cherry trees in their back garden, and we knew how good those cherries would and did taste! Before the dawn fully ascended, we went running into our homes, our stomachs unable to handle the fresh fruit. We were sick all morning, and when our parents found out what we had done, we had to apologize personally to the Tanners and promise never to help ourselves again. Grace Tanner said we could have all we wanted, but just needed to knock on the door and ask! (It was so simple.) But to add insult to injury, my mother decided it would be a good idea for me to go to work for the Hinckleys and pick cherries for them, earn money, and repay the Tanners. So she took us down to the Hinckleys' orchard, and my "pals" and I went up to the Hinckley door and asked if we could have a job picking cherries.

Little did we know that this was a serious fruit farm. President Hinckley (who was always "President Hinckley" to me because he was our stake president) led us out into the orchard and to the trees. We worked all morning and, of course, we weren't even tempted to eat the cherries. All of the Hinckley kids were there as experienced workers, but I had no experience! Sister Hinckley provided drinks and respite to those of us who were not faring so well. After a morning of work, President Hinckley inspected our cherries. My buckets were full, but the stems were not attached. President Hinckley explained to me that this was not acceptable, and that I would have to grab the cherries by the stem and pull from the stem. He said he couldn't sell the cherries that were stemless—too juicy—and I probably should take these cherries home. Now, that was not good. That wasn't what I wanted to hear. Not only did I not want any more cherries, but my morning of hard work was in vain. Instead of earning money, I owed the Hinckleys money! We were only paid for "approved" buckets.

I must have looked very forlorn, because I remember Sister Hinckley at that moment coming over to me, putting her arm around me, and offering me a drink under a shaded tree. I've always thought her face looked like an angel's, but definitely that morning it looked much more so. Because of her nurturing, I was able to continue picking on other mornings to earn enough money to counter my mischief.

Pak Byung Kyu, an early member of the Church in Korea, reflects on the motherliness of Sister Hinckley toward the members:

As far as I remember, Sister Hinckley acted quietly, always with a smile on her face. She looked like a mother or grandmother who always takes tender care of us with love. She makes us comfortable, like my mother. I got an impression that she and President Hinckley are one, well harmonized. She always seems to support President Hinckley quietly and tenderly with beautiful harmony.

Elder Yoshihiko Kikuchi was another of the early Asian Saints who responded to Sister Hinckley's motherliness. He describes his first memory of her:

November 20, 1962, when I was a young missionary in Fukuoka, Japan, I attended a zone conference presided over by Elder Gordon B. Hinckley. I was the only Japanese missionary. We met from early morning until afternoon. Then the sacrament was passed and we had a testimony meeting presided over by Elder Hinckley.

I remember very vividly and clearly, as though it were yesterday, that Sister Marjorie Hinckley stood up to bear her testimony. In her testimony she said, "Heavenly Father loves you; Jesus Christ loves you; and your parents—they love you so much. And, we love you." She gave us more words at that meeting. I could not understand English at that time, but my companion translated her words for me. Sister Hinckley asked all the missionaries to make sure that we wrote home regularly.

I grew up in a single mother's home. My father died during World War II, and my mother was not a member of the Church. But because of Sister Hinckley's words, I decided that day that I would write at least every month and tell my mother how much I loved her and how much I enjoyed serving as a missionary for The Church of Jesus Christ of Latter-day Saints. Making that decision blessed both my mother and me.

I felt a tremendous motherly love from Sister Marjorie Hinckley. I felt her tremendous spirit that day. I thanked the Lord that I had the privilege to meet such a sweet, pure, sincere, beautiful lady in the Church. This caused me to love my own mother more and now also my sweet companion.

Since then I have had the privilege to be with Sister Hinckley many times. But, in fact, the memories and feelings I had in that missionary meeting long ago have never left me.

Patricia P. Pinegar, Primary General President, also describes Sister Hinckley as "motherly":

I became acquainted with Marjorie Hinckley through the eyes of her daughter Virginia Hinckley Pearce.

I was called to serve as second counselor in the Young Women General Presidency in March 1992. Sister Janette Hales Beckham was called to serve as president, Virginia as first counselor, and Carolyn Rasmus was the administrative assistant. Occasionally in our presidency meetings we would share our love and, at times, our concerns for our dear family members. It was through this sharing that I grew to love Marjorie Hinckley. Virginia always spoke of her with such tenderness and love.

One spring day, while Sister Beckham was in a meeting, Virginia, Carolyn, and I went for a walk. We stopped at a shop that was displaying denim hats with sunflowers on them. Feeling in a carefree mood, we each purchased a hat. As we walked back to the office, Virginia suggested we stop by and say hello to her mother. We donned our hats and rang the doorbell. She was delighted to see us, invited us in, exclaimed over our hats, took our pictures, and asked what we girls were up to.

Everything Virginia had told us about her was true. Marjorie Hinckley is warm and quick-witted. She is genuinely interested in each individual she meets. She is unpretentious and just plain good. The highest compliment I could give her would be that she is motherly, a word that embodies all that is good in a woman.

Like that of mothers everywhere, Marjorie Hinckley's compassion constantly reaches out to all children. A daughter-in-law remembers a conversation:

One morning I called to see how Grandma was doing and she said, "I was doing my housework and I felt depressed. I thought, 'Why am I feeling so depressed?' Then I remembered the sad news I had just read about the airline crash. Imagine the grief of all those families. Imagine the children left without fathers and mothers."

Sister Hinckley's philosophy of mothering and homemaking shines clearly in a speech she gave to a group of women:

We have a lot to learn about simplifying our lives. We have to decide what is important and then move along at a pace that is comfortable for us. We have to develop the maturity to stop trying to prove anything, to be what we are. With all of these decisions we have three responsibilities:

We have a great responsibility to our husbands. I know it is hard to believe, but almost before you can turn around the children will be gone and you will be alone with him. You had better be sure that you are developing the kind of love and friendship that will be delightful and enduring. Let the children learn from your attitude that he is important. Encourage him. Be kind. It is a rough world, and he, like everyone else, is fighting to survive. Be cheerful. Don't be a whiner.

Hinckley family

We have a great responsibility to our children. Find joy in them. Don't overschedule them or yourself. You may not be able to take them on exotic vacations. It doesn't matter. When the day dawns bright and sunny, take an excursion to the canyon or park. When it's cloudy and wet, read a book together or make something good to eat. Give them time to explore and learn about the feel of grass and the wiggliness of worms.

Now to our homes. Your home is your own private temple. Keep it clean. Put something beautiful in every room for your family to look at. Create a feeling of order and spirituality. Your home can be beautiful without being elaborate or expensive. I once went tracting with a sister missionary in Hong Kong. We entered the door of a resettlement flat. It was small: four bunk beds, no closets. All the clothes and belongings were stacked neatly on the beds. There was one low table with low stools and an ugly black stove that burned oil. And then my eyes fell on a vase of artificial flowers on a high shelf just under the ceiling. I was touched by that woman's desire for beauty.

As you create a home, don't get distracted with a lot of things that have no meaning for either you or your family. Don't dwell on your failures, but think about your successes.

Have joy in your home.

Have joy in your husband.

Have joy in your children.

Be grateful for the journey.

OPTIMISM

*

"DO WHAT NEEDS TO BE DONE, WHEN IT NEEDS TO BE DONE, WITH A CHEERFUL HEART"

Marjorie (r.) and friend

77

Sister Hinckley loves to tell about her great grandmother Charlotte Hyder Evans, who did nothing spectacular in her life, but simply "did what needed to be done, when it needed to be done, and did it with a cheerful heart." Charlotte's great-granddaughter is a master at doing the same.

Consistently positive, cheerful, and optimistic, Marjorie has an ability to see the good in any situation—and to see it instantly—that makes Pollyanna look like an amateur! The cup is never half-empty, always almost-full or about-to-be-full. With this optimism comes a willingness to be flexible and adaptive, to not overreact to daily irritations. Her basic philosophy is that things always work out somehow.

Shortly before we were to be married, Gordon called and said, "I think we had better go to lunch today." So we did and he said, "I think you should know that I only have $150 to my name." Well, $150 sounded like a small fortune to me. I had hoped for a husband and now I was getting $150 too! I said, "Oh, that will work out just fine; if you've got $150, we're set!"

The following excerpt from a family letter demonstrates Sister Hinckley's example of "doing what needs to be done, when it needs to be done, and with a cheerful heart":

I have been working in the yard (11 hours on Friday). Then went to Jane's until 10 o'clock Saturday night to help her prepare and serve the food and back to the yard for about 7 hours Monday and then to Mother's Monday night for yard clean-up at her place. About 30 posterity showed up and it was a smashing success. The men brought a truck and cleaned up the yard, while the women worked in the house. Dorene made a freezer of homemade ice cream and the little ones had a ball running around with their little rakes and shovels. However, as a result of all this physical activity, when my obligation at Relief Society was over yesterday I bit the dust. I had planned to whip into my long-neglected house, but I got on the sofa and sat there like a zombie. I was bone weary. But after a good night's rest I am fit again and have already done a good-size wash and dug three flats of strawberries and taken them to the neighbors, and since Mrs. LeFevre is coming on Friday to clean the house, I am going back to the yard work. My problem is that I would rather play in the mud than do housework.

P.S. Tomorrow I will be downtown to meet Mother so will take care of your errand at Deseret Book. The other request I will try to get to on Sunday.

Another family letter describes her unquenchable cheerfulness—even about her own failures:

I have a new project, one chapter a day from each of the standard works. I have been on it for four days and am only three days behind. Better to have tried and failed than never to have tried.

Janet Lee, wife of the late Rex E. Lee, former president of Brigham Young University, remembers an occasion when Sister Hinckley's optimistic outlook changed her own perspective:

Several years ago, during the Christmas season, President and Sister Hinckley came to BYU for a musical event. Before the program, there was a buffet dinner, and at one point while the men were away from our table, the women began to talk about the frustrations of getting ready for Christmas. Our conversation focused on the fact that everything about the season was becoming a burden for women. We bear the responsibility of selecting gifts, organizing social events, preparing everyone's favorite food, and making certain that family, guests, and even the less fortunate have a merry Christmas. We felt overwhelmed if not resentful.

Sister Hinckley listened patiently, and then without the slightest edge of criticism in her voice said, "I love Christmas. It is the most joyful of all seasons. I love seeing the eyes of little children light up on Christmas morning. I love giving gifts. I love being with my family. We just need to simplify and remember what we are celebrating."

After she had spoken, something magical happened. Our attitudes shifted, and we began to talk about the birth of our Savior and the spirit of giving. In the years that have passed since those words were spoken, a burden has been lifted for me during the holidays. As I shop, prepare food, and join with friends and family to celebrate the birth of our Savior, her words nurture and calm me. "I love Christmas," I hear her say, and I let her teach me to relax and enjoy the season.

Hobie Hinckley, a grandson, remarks on Sister Hinckley's good cheer:

If you're feeling down about anything, it's difficult to stay so for long when you're with her. She has such a contagious smile that cheers you right up. Her laugh and the way she talks about things makes you feel like she sees the bright side of everything.

Jessica Dudley, a granddaughter, agrees:

If you're having a bad day, five minutes with Grandma's never-failing optimism will make you wonder why you were feeling sorry for yourself in the first place.

Another granddaughter, Katie B. Wright, says:

I have never seen Grandma mad or sad. She is always so pleasant and happy. I love her SO much and I am so happy that she is my Grandma!

Roger Dudley, a son-in-law, describes her as the "Ever-Positive, Never-Bad-Day Grandma":

Grandma Hinckley is truly one of a kind. I look forward to Grandma's visits to "the little house" in East Millcreek. She greets us with a warm, friendly smile and "How are you today?" or "What's new in your life?" She listens to the answer and responds as if you and your concerns are all that matter to her. Every day is the "most gorgeous day" or "such a wonderful day." Never a negative, always a positive word from Grandma Hinckley.

On one occasion my wife and I met her parents in New York, where we attended a thrilling 24,000-member meeting at Madison Square Garden. The high point of the two-hour meeting was little Grandma Hinckley standing a tall four-foot-eight (maybe) at the rostrum, peering over the pulpit and saying, "Hello." That simple but love-tendered introduction melted the members in the huge Madison Square arena. From the very start she had them in her hand, and their expressions showed a deep and abiding love for her. Likewise, at a subsequent missionary meeting held at the Manhattan chapel, Grandma Hinckley began with that simple but warm icebreaker, "Hello, I know you and love you." Instantly every missionary was sitting at the feet of his own grandma. Every word was positive and uplifting, based on a deep sense of love and concern for their well-being.

As we traveled to Salt Lake from New York, I had occasion to watch Grandma Hinckley as she tried to sleep or get comfortable to ease her leg pains. With her eyes closed, often her face grimaced in pain. But when asked about her pain, she said, "It was worth every minute to be with the members and missionaries. It was such a wonderful day." Regardless of the length of the meeting or the car or airplane ride, it is always a wonderful day for Grandma Hinckley.

Duane Cardall, a television reporter, interviewed Sister Hinckley shortly after her husband was ordained President of the Church. He comments on her cheerful support of her husband's grueling schedule:

"Everything is okay" in her mind, even though the couple's

81

schedule of public appearances and frequent travel is extraordinarily challenging, especially for people their age. It is common for the news media and others to comment about the President's grueling schedule "at an age when most men are well into retirement," sometimes forgetting that she is regularly there at his side, supporting him and fulfilling her providential role as the eternal companion to one of God's chosen servants. "Trying to keep up" may be a real concern for a woman in her eighties, simply because of the physical demands of being the wife of the President of The Church of Jesus Christ of Latter-day Saints. But, certainly, she never "just goes along."

"We have a good life," she said as we concluded our television interview. "We love it. We love what we're doing. I wouldn't change a thing. Not a thing."

Barbara Ballard, wife of Elder M. Russell Ballard of the Twelve, has often traveled with the Hinckleys on assignments. She remarks:

I have seen Sister Hinckley when she is very tired during the activities of an assignment overseas and other places. Someone will want to show her something or speak to her. She will perk right up and, with her big smile and twinkling eyes, say, "I'm loving every minute of it." And she is!

Even when expressing honest discouragement, Sister Hinckley is optimistic, and it shows. In a letter to a daughter who was moving to a new home out of state, she wrote:

I was an absolute basket case last night after saying good-bye to Clark and his little family and then saying good-bye to you and yours and leaving you both in overwhelming situations and then to come home to this echoing silence and find the notes left by the girls. It was all too much. To top it off, there was no answer at Dudleys or Pearces and a busy signal at Dick's which lasted the entire night. Either they have left the receiver off or their German guest was spending an evening at home. In desperation I called Evelyn just to tell someone that I was home, but she had taken Amy and all her little friends to the cabin for the night. I finally got Aunt Ruth and she was a sympathetic listener while I told her about how cruel life is. Then I felt better. Dad kept assuring me that you are young and that somehow, before too long, you would both be settled into a respectable house and have an interesting lifestyle going. I know it is all true, but yesterday it looked bleak.

I kept thinking yesterday that you are right back where you were when you arrived in Hawaii two years ago, and you came out in beautiful style there and you will do the same in Chicago—it is just that the pattern is becoming monotonous. It is like climbing a mountain and as soon as you reach the top you get knocked back down to the bottom to climb it again, but I guess the fun is in climbing and not in arriving.

Steven C. Bennion, president of Southern Utah University, remembers the Hinckleys from his childhood days:

While Marjorie Hinckley would shun adulation or worldly honors, her own optimism, cheerful outlook, and good humor make it difficult to remember anything but these overriding positive traits that have been such a blessing to her family and those around her. She is a joy! She is not a person given to self-pity, even though she could find things to feel sorry about in her condition if she chose to. I never remember that being part of her response to difficulties or challenges.

Augusto Lim, an early Filipino convert, remembers:

Sister Hinckley would go out of her way to shake our hands and embrace us, and she always kissed my wife. She was so easy to be with, so caring and loving and concerned about our mutual friends as well as our own welfare.

Han In Sang, an early member of the Church in Korea, recalls the visits of the Hinckleys during the early 1960s:

We didn't have any decent hotels in Korea so it was a tremendous sacrifice for them [Elder and Sister Hinckley] to come. Sometimes they would sleep at the mission home. We didn't have a boiler system, so we would heat water on a big kettle for them to use. Sister Hinckley never complained. In fact, she made us feel as though what we had to offer was a palace. In return, she always brought several pounds of chocolates to give to the missionaries and members.

Do what needs to be done, when it needs to be done, and do it with a cheerful heart. She preaches what she practices in a note to a granddaughter on the eve of starting junior high school:

Dearest Cede,
   Tomorrow you will be starting out to conquer a new world. Tuck this $5.00 in your pocket. You may need a bottle of glue to keep yourself together, or to keep your smile glued on. Good luck! We are so proud of you.
   Love,
   Grams

Ultimately, Sister Hinckley's advice to college students expresses the way she lives her own life:

Think about your particular assignment at this time in your life. It is to get an education. This is a wonderful assignment. Don't take it lightly. Give it your full heart and energy. Do whatever you have to do this week; do it with all your heart and soul; and do it cheerfully. To do less than this will leave you with an empty feeling.

Marjorie about the time of her marriage, 1937

CHAPTER FIVE

GRATITUDE

*

"I DON'T KNOW WHY I HAVE BEEN SO BLESSED"

I am so grateful for the blessings that I have enjoyed in my life. I do not know why the Lord has been so good to me. I don't know why I have been so blessed. But I do know that the Lord has a right to expect a lot of me. Sometimes the commitment gets a little heavy and sometimes I wonder if I can really do this. Then I think of all that I have been given, and it is easy to get up and do a little something more.

Marjorie Hinckley seems to be missing a piece—a piece we call "entitlement." Her children have always laughed at her motto: "Expect the worst, and if it doesn't happen, you'll be pleasantly surprised!" She has spent most of her life "pleasantly surprised" and incredibly grateful.

Characteristically humble, Sister Hinckley is quick to see her own weaknesses. A pair of family letters give insight into her humble and grateful heart:

Last Thursday at [the General Authorities'] Wives luncheon two of the granddaughters of Susa Young Gates gave a musical skit of her life. She was a prolific writer, do-good-er, organizer, etc., etc., etc. I turned to Sister Kimball and said, "It makes me wonder what I am doing with my life." "You are running to and fro," she quipped. She was right. I am running to and fro and shiver to think that someday I will have to account for the time spent.

*****

Wednesday after work Dad and I came home by way of the grocery store to get some milk. It was six o'clock, the dinner hour. A little boy about eight years old was ahead of me in the line. He meekly pushed a worn and torn food stamp coupon across the counter and said his mother wanted to know if he could get a can of soup with it. The clerk told him that he could not spend a food coupon that had been torn out of the book, and he went away empty-handed. It wasn't until I got out to the car that I realized that perhaps he was actually hungry with no food in the house. It has haunted me ever since. I don't know why I didn't have the presence of mind to take him back in the store and buy him a bag of groceries. Needless to say, I have eaten every meal since with a little more gratitude. Sometimes I forget that everyone does not live so well.

Marjorie often says that whatever is good about her mothering, she learned from her mother. To take care of the "guilt" on Mother's Day, she simply thinks about her own mother and grandmothers with gratitude.

As I see traits of Mother coming out in my children and grandchildren, I am constantly having to say, "Thank you,

87

Mother, for what you were, for your faith which has gone down into the very bones of your posterity."

In her private conversation and public speaking, Sister Hinckley's ever-grateful heart constantly finds expression. The following tender words of gratitude were given to a group of student nurses in 1962:

As I sat through your opening exercises this morning, the beatitude came into my mind that says, "Blessed are they who hunger and thirst after righteousness, for they shall be filled." You are they who hunger and thirst after righteousness or you certainly would not have bothered to come here this morning. You were under no obligation. I love you for coming. Every time I see a group of young people such as you I feel as if I would like to lay the world at your feet if it were in my power to do so. But it is not within my power to give you anything. Only as the Lord blesses this gathering with His Spirit will we gain anything at all by meeting together.

I could not have refused this invitation if I had wanted to when I learned that this was to be a meeting of BYU student nurses. It was six years ago this week that I came to the hospital for a serious operation. For two weeks I was in a fog. Of all the faces that went in and out of my room during those days, the only one that I have any distinct remembrance of was a girl in a blue uniform who said that she was a BYU student nurse. I remember her red hair, and her kindly face, but most of all the compassion and tenderness that I felt in her hands. I knew she was trying to help me. With some of the others I had serious doubts. By the time I was well enough to make her acquaintance she had been transferred. The first day up I wheeled myself to a window at the north end of the corridor, and I saw her leaving this home with a fine-looking boy. She was dressed in her Sunday best. I have often wondered what became of her. One thing I am sure of, that if she pursued her nursing career, she is a very, very good nurse.

Norma Ashton, wife of the late Elder Marvin J. Ashton and longtime friend of Marjorie's, comments:

Her expressions of gratitude and appreciation for the smallest to the greatest deeds of service come from her lips to build and acknowledge love for the givers.

Sister Hinckley suggests that remembering and counting blessings creates happiness:

Last evening we took our children walking around the ski trails in Little Cottonwood Canyon. I began to go over in my mind anything that I could think of that had brought inspiration into my life during the past year. There have been numerous experiences that have filled my heart with gratitude. There have been people I have met who have lifted me to a plane of greater endeavor, books I have read that have left their mark.

It's a valuable exercise to close your eyes every once in a while and think, "What is the most wonderful moment I have lived through during the past year?" I immediately think of two wonderful moments. One is when Evan Harbrecht's beautiful voice filled the Swiss Temple on dedication day with the strains of "Bless This House." Another was just an offhand remark from my nineteen-year-old boy when he said, "Gee, thanks, Mom," as

I handed him a freshly ironed shirt. The grand and the simple. They are equally wonderful.

Several years later, Sister Hinckley spoke of the same exercise—looking back and remembering wonderful experiences with gratitude.

I don't know why I have had so many wonderful experiences, but I do know how grateful I am for them. I am especially grateful for all of the temple dedications I've participated in. Those are always wonderful events. One of the most impressive temple dedications that I ever went to was in Peru. I will never forget those beautiful people coming down out of the hills with their black braids down their backs; the women in brilliant, flowered skirts, holding white handkerchiefs in one hand and their temple recommends in the other hand.

So when I go to bed and I can't go to sleep, I don't count sheep; I think of these beautiful experiences that I have had. I am so grateful for each one.

Sister Hinckley admonishes young adults to cultivate a grateful heart:

A grateful heart will give you a touch of refinement that can come in no other way.

I went to high school during the days of the famous Depression. It was a miserable experience. But, in a way, I wish you could have been there with us. Somehow it helped me to appreciate much more the prosperity we now enjoy. I know some of you think you are on a tight budget, and you are. I am glad if you are. But it is a tight budget because you have nothing else to compare with it. It isn't your fault that you have had three square meals a day, most every day of your life. It isn't your fault that you have never been hungry in your life. It isn't your fault that somehow or other you have always been able to get a new pair of shoes, whether you needed them or not. It isn't your fault that you have at least five or six changes of clothing in your crowded closets. But all of this makes it doubly hard for you to be truly grateful.

Has the fear of not being able to get an education ever struck terror into your heart? Probably not, for you knew that somehow or other you would get here and that somehow or other you will stay as long as you so desire, for this is America, where only your own indolence can keep you from the good things of life.

And when you finally develop a little gratitude in your heart, make up your mind to express it. "Appreciation unexpressed is not appreciation." If you can't find someone to say thank you to for something, just take a look at your toothbrush and say, "Thank you for being. You are a wonderful little gadget."

"Thank you" is a wonderful phrase. Use it. It will add stature to your soul. Never let a day go by without saying thank you to someone for something—and especially to your Heavenly Father.

Heidi P. Jenson, a granddaughter, recalls the effects of her grandmother's appreciative attitude:

I never considered my mom's cooking good *or* bad until Grandma came for dinner one day. "Your mother is such a good cook!" she said. "Oh, this food is delicious." I had to say to myself,

"Hmm. This food is pretty good." Grandma is always so appreciative, and it's contagious.

In a 1964 interview with Dorothy O. Rea of the Church News, *Sister Hinckley emphasized the importance of gratitude:*

It has been a matter of concern to me as I have seen the luxury of America compared to other lands. I have wondered how we can teach gratitude and humility to our American children in the face of such abundance. Perhaps the best way is to be constant in the matter of family prayer.

It is good to kneel as a family and to hear daily expressions of gratitude to our Heavenly Father for the blessings we enjoy. The Lord intended His children to enjoy the good things of life. With all that we have, we must also have grateful hearts. We must teach our children not to take all that they have for granted.

In 1954, she spoke in a sacrament meeting on the same topic:

When I was young, a Sunday School teacher once faced our class and said, "I would like to tell you what I am thankful for. I am thankful for my home. I am thankful that I have a good husband and children. I am thankful that I have enough money for the comforts of life." And many other things she listed. "But most of all," she said, "I am grateful for the trials I have had."

This sounded strange to us young people, but as the years have gone by I have come to know what she meant. For it is the trials of life that make us humble and make us strong. I could list bounteous material blessings that the Lord has showered down upon me in this past year. But I am most grateful of all for the small trials that were mine. I am grateful that the Lord in his

wisdom saw fit to deprive me of my health and strength for a suf-
ficient length of time that I came to appreciate what good health
means and what joy there is in being able to do a day's honest
work. And I have now come to sympathize and understand better the discouragement of the sick among us. I came to know
what the love of a neighbor and goodness of a friend can mean
in time of need. I am indeed grateful that there have been a few
times in my life that I have had to depend entirely on the Lord
for my well-being and comfort.

The road has not been paved all the way for any of us. We
all have a small place in our hearts where we store our sorrows
and disappointments. But are there not days when you are simply
overwhelmed with the blessings of the Lord?

It was ever thus. Nephi said it well: "I, Nephi, having been
born of goodly parents . . . having seen many afflictions in the
course of my days, nevertheless, having been highly favored of
the Lord in all my days" (1 Nephi 1:1).

I can only thank my Father in Heaven for wonderful and
unusual opportunities. I know that where much is given, much is
expected. And that is a frightening
thought.

Ruth Faust, wife of President James E.
Faust and a dear friend and neighbor,
comments on Sister Hinckley's constant
expressions of gratitude:

In our conversations, Marjorie
always acknowledges the blessings
of the Lord in her life. She indeed

has a grateful heart. Not only is she grateful for the wonderful husband that she married but for her children, grandchildren, and great-grandchildren as well. Many times I have heard her mention what a blessing it is for her to meet the devoted Saints all over the world when she travels with her husband. She feels it a great privilege to be a member of this church. She is grateful for her health, her heritage, and for the happiness in her heart.

A letter to a missionary granddaughter just before her release is a final, crowning example of Sister Hinckley's humility and gratitude:

So, time is running out, but you still have your life ahead of you. For me, time is running out—period. And I also have the feeling: what have I done?! There is still so much to do and so little time. I am grateful for every day.

Marjorie, about 1934

ENTHUSIASM
FOR LEARNING

*

"MAKE LIFE AN ADVENTURE"

Make life an adventure. Don't say, "Well, here's another day." Say, "Here's a new day. What have I that I can put into it?"

One of Marjorie Hinckley's most contagious qualities is her boundless fascination with new people, new information, strange sights and sounds. Life is a wonderful adventure to her, and to be in her presence is to suddenly see it all that way.

She is an eager reader. Devouring biographies, great literature, the latest best-seller, or a wonderful new children's book, she always has new ideas to talk about.

When asked in an interview if she ever imagined where her life would take her, Sister Hinckley responded with typical enthusiasm:

I didn't. I was busy getting through today. But I didn't think much about where I was going to go or what was going to happen. I didn't give it a lot of thought. It is amazing. I sometimes have to pinch myself a little, thinking about what I've seen and experienced. It never gets old; I just can't believe what's going on. Every day is so exciting. When you see what's happening with the Church, you just get up thrilled every morning, wanting to shout, "Oh, wow, this is so good!"

Elder Bruce Hafen of the Seventy describes her eagerness for knowledge:

Marjorie Hinckley's outlook is intellectually enlarging. She has actively nourished a lifelong development of her own mind and gifts. She has been an avid reader, always reading to her children and for herself. When one of her children enrolled in a university literature class, she signed up and audited the entire course. For years she has regularly enrolled in LDS institute classes. Her natural gift for writing has produced precious bundles of family letters and biographical sketches.

She is curious, observant, thoughtful, and aesthetically sensitive. She remembers with great appreciation the painting of the boy Jesus her mother placed in her bedroom, where the "first thing I saw each morning was his beautiful face." She admired Camilla Kimball for taking up oil painting at age ninety-two. And she loves recalling that it was the rich voice of John Taylor singing a hymn that attracted her great-grandfather to hear the gospel in England 150 years ago.

Sister Hinckley tells of her own "self-directed" education:

I had hoped to go to the University of Utah. But the year was 1929, "the bottom of the Depression." On the day I registered for classes, I returned home to find that the company my father had been working for as an accountant had gone bankrupt and closed. He was out of work. The next day I withdrew from the university, went downtown, and miraculously secured a job as a secretary. Since college was not an option, I decided, well, if this is my life, I'd better educate myself. And I worked hard at it. I read and I read and I read.

This habit has been a blessing to her posterity, as Jennie H. Soulier, a granddaughter, explains:

Grandma loves to read. When I received my mission call to Rome, she said, "You must read *The Agony and the Ecstasy*, by Irving Stone. You will love it and appreciate the greatness of Rome even more."

Sister Hinckley admonishes college students to study and learn.

Is it worthwhile to be an excellent student? I think it is. The Lord gave you a brain. He intended that you use it. Most of us never get beyond 30 percent of our capabilities. The thing that motivates me is the knowledge that I am a spirit child of God. Because we are His children, we must resemble our Heavenly Father. Do your best. Learn everything you can. The day may come when you will need it.

Everything you do now is preparing you for something else. Did you know that?

Brother Hinckley studied English at the university. He wondered why. Now he knows. When I was a child my parents had me take elocution lessons. How I hated it. But I believe that largely because of those dreaded lessons, I have been able to stand before thousands of people and speak the thoughts of my heart without shaking to death!

How blessed will your children be if you develop some intellectual curiosity. And you will never be bored. God is what He is because He knows everything. And the beautiful thing about it, and one of the things I love most about the gospel, is that everything we learn we can use and take with us and use again. What a concept!

Celia B. Benson, a granddaughter, remembers:

At my wedding shower Grandma gave me an iron with a card that read, "Happy ironing! The most enjoyable of all household duties. Love, Grandma H." It reminded me of when I was trying to decide on a major in college. Grandma told me to study something other than home economics so that when I was at home doing the ironing I would have something interesting to think about. Now, when I pull my old iron off the shelf and run it over a wrinkled blouse, I think of sonnets and Shakespeare . . . and I think of Grandma and smile.

Sister Hinckley's love of learning endeared her to others of like mind. Steve Bennion, a neighbor, says:

When my family moved to East Mill Creek (in the 1940s) it was part of the beginnings of suburban development in the southeastern part of the Salt Lake Valley. Homes were slowly springing up, closer together than had been the earlier pattern when they were surrounded by farms. Seeking a small farm of his own, my father, Lowell Bennion, moved his family to a four-acre plot adjacent to the Hinckleys' farm. Even though the Hinckley and Bennion homes by street were about three blocks apart, in that setting we were comparatively close neighbors. My mother, Merle Colton Bennion, was not as excited to come to the country, since they were leaving a home across the street from the University of Utah and all of the cultural advantages that this close proximity provided.

One of the very precious silver linings in this move to East Mill Creek for my mother was her new neighbor, Marjorie Hinckley. In her she found an instant friend. They had the common bonds of being young mothers quite removed from shopping and other conveniences. There were no bus lines that far in the country in those days, and generally only one family vehicle.

But even more than these commonalities, in Marjorie Hinckley my mother found someone with many common interests. They both loved to read, and they talked about great books they shared. Her innate curiosity and love of learning never waned.

An excerpt from a 1978 family letter shows Marjorie's enthusiasm for learning as well as her disarming humility:

Am taking another great class at the Institute, but instead of going early in the morning it is at 1:10. Much easier than those early morning classes. The teacher graduated in theater and every class is like a "G"-rated movie. *The Ten Commandments* was a drag compared to the show he puts on. I must say he makes the Book of Mormon come alive. I can't believe what I miss when I read the scriptures on my own.

Sister Hinckley's letters home to her children were always a detailed and wonder-filled recital of her adventures in the world.

For a place to see [Korea] is a clock stopper. And I guess we looked as curious to them as they did to us. Every time we would stop, a dozen children and old folks would gather around to stare, so everyone was staring at everyone. Their native dress is so different—everything from white blouse pants like the Egyptians to beautiful satin brocade coats worn by the women over six or seven layers of long johns and sweaters and other clothing. Women walking down the streets with big jars of water balancing on their heads, oxen drawing big loads of bricks, men carrying huge pieces of furniture on A-frames on their backs. The whole thing was a sight to behold.

Jennie H. Soulier, a granddaughter, comments on this irrepressible enthusiasm for other places and cultures:

My favorite attribute of Grandma is her enthusiasm for life and for all the different, wonderful people in it. She has made me so excited to learn all about others, and enjoy all the different places there are in the world. It's true! I have loved living in different places and loving the people there, just as she said. And each time I go back to Salt Lake, we always have a wonderful catch-up time on all that is happening.

Sister Hinckley describes her feelings about travel:

Travel is wonderful, but sometimes it gets to be a blur—even gets old. But when you get there with the people, you come alive! The people are so wonderful.

There are so many places and people that I have come to love.

I love Hong Kong. I think Hong Kong is one of the most interesting cities in the world. There are two cultures there—

there's the British culture and the Chinese culture—all living together. The city itself, of course, is just fascinating. People live on the street, they cook their meals on the street, they sleep on the street. And you're in it. You don't have to go to their homes, or you don't have to just wonder what it's like in their private lives, because their private lives are on the sidewalk.

I love London, too. It's one of my favorite cities in the whole wide world.

I love to go to Korea, anyplace in Korea. I think it's the people that I love there. We have seen so much history in their country. After the war, the trees were gone. They cut them down to burn in their stoves. They were living in shanties. They would get an old piece of corrugated iron and mount it up to make four walls. They are great people—so resilient.

I love to try new things. Including food. But I have never acquired a taste for kim-chee. It's the only food that I've ever run into that I couldn't enjoy. I told that to one of the Korean members, and he said: "Well, it's just as good as your blue cheese dressing." Maybe so!

Maxine Grimm, a longtime friend who lived in the Philippines during the early days of the Church there, describes Marjorie's enthusiasm:

I well remember Marjorie Hinckley's early visits to the Philippines. One day I took her to a very typical Philippine market. It was all under one roof and housed everything from live chickens, pigs, and fish to rice, corn, vegetables, raw sugar, exotic fruits, pots, pans, dishes, linens, embroidered tablecloths, crocheted articles, and so on. It is unbelievable the things you can find. I loved Marjorie's reaction—she squealed as an eel slithered out of its basket and a boy went racing after it—she returned smiles to the many vendors who recognized us as potential customers—"Mum, we have special new cloth, you see"—and she bargained right along with me for a table-cloth. Filipinos love to bargain and are even known to bargain away their profit. Marjorie bought a tablecloth, which she says she still uses on special occasions, and other articles for gifts for her family. We left dripping with perspiration but laughing, and Marjorie commented that this was the first time she had ever been in a market with live chickens.

Postcards to grandchildren were filled with the excitement of new places and people.

Heidi P. Jenson, a granddaughter, has other pleasant memories of her grandmother's travels:

As children, we loved to visit Grandma after she had been on a trip. We would run into her bedroom and she would throw open her suitcase. And then the little presents would flow: peanuts and eye-blinders and winged pens—oh, the delights!—small toothbrushes, combs, mouthwash, and soap. Then we would follow her into the family room, where she would be telling our mothers every detail of the meetings, the sights, and the people. I've been over the world and back through Grandma's stories.

Another granddaughter, Angela B. Folsom, describes how Grandma Hinckley's enthusiasm for faraway places has blessed her own life:

Several years ago my husband was asked by his company to move to Tokyo, Japan. Although my husband had served a mission in Japan, we had never talked of the possibility of someday moving there. While we were prayerfully deciding if this was right for our family, I had many personal questions of my own: How would I communicate? Could I be happy in such a foreign country? Could I adjust to the culture? Most of the questions I couldn't answer, but as we made the decision to move, I realized I was more excited than frightened. Yes, it was a frightening experience I had ahead of me, but all my life I had heard fascinating stories of the Saints in Asia, and I was excited to become a part of it.

One of my vivid memories is of going to Grandma and Grandpa Hinckley's as a child during general conference weekend. The house was always full of Saints from all over the world. Grandma opened her home to those people, and they had wonderful reunions. I remember one Chinese lady (I think from Hong Kong) in particular who visited quite often. She always made egg foo yong in Grandma's kitchen, and I couldn't figure out why it never tasted like the "Americanized" Chinese food from our favorite Chinese restaurant.

Grandma always had wonderful Asian souvenirs in her home.

The Japanese rice bowls, the Taiwanese bamboo plates, the Philippine shell placemats were all things I considered treasures. Certainly there was a mystique about the countries from which such wonderful things were acquired. Along with the tangible objects were the stories she shared of the wonder of these countries and the faithful Saints living there. She broadened my horizons and made the world a much smaller place through her stories. Through the stories of her travels, she brought the world into focus.

Thus, when I thought about the idea of living in Japan, it didn't seem so foreign to me. There was a familiarity in it. I felt like I knew something of the country already.

We have now had the opportunity as a family to travel to many of the Asian countries I heard so much about as a child. I now have my own set of Japanese rice bowls, Philippine shell placemats, and Hong Kong pearls. These treasures remind me of Grandma and her love of both the countries and, more especially, the people around the world.

Jessica Dudley, a granddaughter, recognizes that same quality of love:

There is a sparkle of magic that glows from Grandma. It is a love of life, a love of people, a love of the gospel. It is wonderful, almost mystical. It is natural for her, but feels anything but natural to the rest of the world. Grandma shares her magic with everyone, while at the same time, she makes you feel like you are the special one she chose to share it with.

Learning, growing, and loving have been lifelong pursuits for Marjorie Hinckley. Her encouraging advice to a group of students bespeaks her own commitment to intellectual interests:

When I was a young girl I read the autobiography of Benjamin Franklin. It affected me greatly. It is a book about goals. Whether or not Mr. Franklin actually carried out in detail all the ways of living that he listed is not important to me. The inspiring thing to me was that early in life he decided on some goals. They were specific. Somehow I have the feeling that life is so short that unless we begin now to organize and plan, it is going to slip away in bits and pieces with nothing ever realized.

What a world to live in! Never has there been so much to read just to keep up on world affairs. Never has there been so much to learn. Never has there been so much music to listen to. When I was in high school there used to be a ward dance every Thursday night. We walked to the church and when we turned the corner on 8th East we could hear the orchestra and we would break into a run, so excited were we to hear the music. It was just about the only music we heard from Thursday to Thursday, outside of the two or three phonograph records we owned—one of Caruso and the other a violin solo by Kreisler. Now I move from room to room in our small home, and I can hear music from every corner. What a world!

I remember a day when one of my sons read seven history books for a test in history. For three or four days preceding the test he neglected every other facet of his life preparing for the test. He went to the test in full confidence. He knew all there was to know about the history of the U.S. from 1914 to 1945. That afternoon he came home with that dazed after-test look in his eyes. "How could it be, Mother? I knew enough on the subject to write a book, but still there were things on that test I didn't know. How much is there to learn in this world? Do you think anyone will ever learn all that he needs to know?" My only answer to that is that it is a good thing eternity is a long time.

When my second son was in high school he came rushing into the house from school one day and said, "Hey, Mom, I learned the neatest thing today. Watch this." His chalk flew across my kitchen blackboard as he worked out a problem in trigonometry. "Did you know that trig is the only branch of math about which you can learn everything there is to know?" he said. Praise be to a teacher who had aroused such a curiosity in a boy that for one brief moment, at least, he was on fire.

Sometimes I think this is what makes the difference between a good student and a poor one. Just a little curiosity. If you have it, cultivate it—hold fast to it. Never let it go. If you do not have it—get it. It is just that simple.

The rewards for intellectual curiosity are many.

The world will always be your pumpkin, full of magic, full of wonder.

You will be interesting to your friends, to your husband, and a joy to your children.

You will have perpetual youth.

CHAPTER
SEVEN

SENSE OF HUMOR

*

"THE ONLY WAY TO GET THROUGH LIFE IS TO LAUGH YOUR WAY THROUGH IT"

Marjorie with Kathleen and Richard

107

Elder Neal A. Maxwell once said, "We are here in mortality, and the only way to go is through; there isn't any around!" (*Ensign*, May 1988, p. 9.) I would add, the only way to get through life is to laugh your way through it.

You either have to laugh or cry. I prefer to laugh. Crying gives me a headache.

Family and friends as well as members of the Church around the world delight in Sister Hinckley's ever-ready sense of humor. The death of President Howard W. Hunter was difficult for her. In addition to the personal loss of a beloved friend, she knew that her life would never be the same. Her sister

Dorene Lloyd called and said, "Marge, how are you feeling?" In a characteristic attempt to lighten the mood, Marjorie said, "I have just been sitting here wondering how a nice girl like me got into a mess like this."

George H. Durham II, a longtime friend of the Hinckleys, says:

My mother (Eudora Widtsoe Durham) was a widow the last ten years of her life. Sister Hinckley continued to be her loving and consistent friend. They often sat together at the monthly General Authorities' Wives luncheon. They continued to see each other at Windsor Club. They spoke with each other on the phone several times a week sometimes. It was a common event for Mother to report to us that she had participated in a wonderful conversation with Sister Hinckley—Marge. When Sister Hinckley spoke at my mother's funeral, she recalled some of these conversations: "Eudora loved her children and grandchildren and was very proud of them. I know all of their virtues. I heard them over and over again!"

Colleen Maxwell, wife of Elder Neal A. Maxwell of the Twelve, recalls a talk Sister Hinckley gave at a regional conference:

She observed that sometimes as she is doing her housework the thought occurs to her of the reality that she is married to the prophet of the Lord. She hastened to add that her first reaction is to think, "I want my mother!"

She also gently teases President Hinckley when he adjusts the microphone for her at meetings as she addresses a congregation, saying, "That's why I bring him along."

Jennie H. Soulier, a granddaughter, remembers another regional conference where her grandmother was asked to speak:

It was a huge stadium full of people. You would think she would be nervous, but she walked up there with all the confidence in the world. She told everyone what it's like to live with a prophet: "He leaves his towels on the floor, and his tie over the couch." She instantly had everyone laughing. I wanted her to go on and on. It's like Grandpa always says, "She steals the show." One of the reasons people like Grandpa so much is because Grandma can win anyone over with her humor.

A postcard from Hong Kong to a grandchild shows her appreciation for the humor inherent even in misunderstandings:

May 15, 1980
Dear Rosemary,

I ordered a hamburger at McDonald's in Hong Kong and told them I wanted a plain bun without sesame seeds. They served me a plain bun with no hamburger and a little catsup! Our Chinese and their English is not all that good.

Hong Kong is more crowded than ever, but just as exciting as always.

Love,
G. Hinckley

Barbara Ballard, wife of Elder M. Russell Ballard of the Twelve, says:

I delight in her terrific sense of humor, which is always based on such practical experiences. She is quite disarming. I recall one missionary meeting in which she could not reach the microphone and the pulpit could not be adjusted. The mission president hurriedly found something for her to stand on. She stepped up, stood tall, looked right out at the missionaries, and said, "Oh my, I've always wondered how it would feel to actually see over the pulpit."

Another time she was in exactly the same predicament at a regional conference. After the "arrangement" was made, she stood, saying, "In my next life I'm going to be 5'8" instead of 4'10"!" These witty comments coming from this adorable lady bring such a joyous response from her audience and endear her to them forever.

Sister Hinckley opened a sacrament meeting talk in November 1954 with the following words:

It is strange how much a woman can find to say when she is leaning on the back fence and how speechless she can become when leaning on the pulpit.

But her humor is more than a pulpit trick. In a family letter, she handles the everyday stresses of life with a light touch:

Saturday we went out to Jane's again to work on the shower. It has become a monumental task. We thought we were getting rid of the old house, but not so. When we got home I had left a pan of spaghetti with hamburger boiling away on the stove. The house was full of thick air and pungent smell. While Dad threw open the windows, I opened the garage door from the kitchen and found that he had pulled the hose inside with the spray sprinkler on and had absentmindedly turned on the tap. Water was hitting the ceiling and spraying from wall to wall to wall. I simply cracked up. We looked at each other in total disbelief and wondered whatever was going to become of us. Like President Clark used to say, "Old age is a blankety blank-blank." We opened up the windows, swept out the water, and decided to get away from it all by going over to see Clark and Kathleen and getting some groceries. While en route I was seized with a sudden pain and hardly made it through the check stand. By the time I got home and into bed I was having chills and fever and was in so much pain that I was trying to decide just what I wanted included in my obituary. Dad called Clark, Kathleen, Jim, and Ginny and told them the invitation to Sunday dinner was off, and that was our Saturday. A great day.

In responding to a comment about her children's sense of humor, she said:

The children learned that from their father. He doesn't take himself seriously either. He takes the things he does seriously, the things that need to be serious, then he's very serious. But he doesn't take himself seriously at all.

Perhaps the times when Sister Hinckley's sense of humor most endears her to others is when she teases her famous husband. The humor is so full of fun and goodness—never hiding any sharp message—that we all join in the laughter, President Hinckley laughing the loudest.

Someone asked Sister Hinckley what it was like being married to the President of the Church. She promptly answered with a twinkle in her eye, "Some days are better than others." And she commented once during an interview:

I've said to my husband more than once, "If you keep trying, you'll be as good a speaker as your father." Gordon just laughs.

Sister Hinckley pokes fun at herself equally often:

When I was sixteen I went to San Francisco on the bus with my girlfriend for a week's vacation. I thought I had seen the

world. Little did I know what the future would hold! We were so naïve. The tour guide took us to a seafood place along the coast, and he said, "If anyone wants to get out here and have a fish cocktail, that would be all right." My friend and I looked at each other and said, "Cocktail! We'll just sit on the bus!" That's how naïve I was.

A daughter-in-law repeats a typical bit of humor:

Recently I picked Grandma up at her apartment for an appointment we had together. I love these moments one-on-one with her. I began telling her about something I had forgotten to do, and said, "I don't know what is happening to me lately. Sometimes, I think I am losing my mind." She quipped, "I know what you mean. I've looked high and low for mine, and I can't find it anywhere!"

The benefits of Sister Hinckley's "disarming humor" are displayed in these thoughts from her daughter Kathleen H. Barnes:

I always assumed that motherhood would be easy. As the oldest child, I had watched Mother welcome each subsequent new baby into our family. It appeared to me to be an occasion that was unequaled in this life. Mother's ease with her children led me to believe that all of motherhood was joy, bliss, and complete satisfaction. She would tell me that the experience of childbirth was akin to dipping into heaven for a brief moment and returning with this blessed new infant. She said that with each new baby came a bundle of love so love never ran thin. She told me that the greatest joys in life were those associated with your children. It appeared to be all true.

When our youngest sister was born, I was ecstatic. I would jump off the school bus each school afternoon and run all the way home, so anxious was I to get home to the new baby. I held her and dressed her and fed her and bathed her. I took her for walks, and when she fussed I handed her to Mother. I agreed with Mother. Having a baby of your own would be the best!

Is it any wonder then, that my intense hunger for my own baby started immediately after I was married? I would often imagine my day with a baby in it. I would see myself holding a baby, dressing a baby, cooing to a baby, loving a baby. I could hardly wait till my dream came true. But, as that blessed state of impending motherhood descended upon me, I found myself sick! Very sick! I couldn't eat or even smell anything that resembled food. I couldn't wake up, and slept night and day. My head was continually in a fog. This was not the way I had pictured it.

The night this first little infant was born didn't exactly feel like a trip to heaven. It was long, miserable, and something I vowed I would never repeat. When she finally arrived, I thought the hard part was over and from this moment forward, the bliss part of motherhood would begin.

Wrong. I took the baby home, thinking the routine of my life would quickly be resumed. My fantasies of dressing her in bows and lace were just around the corner. She was so cute—in fact, she was beautiful. This was going to be great after all.

But I was ill prepared for what I faced. This tiny little six-pound bundle instantly took total control of my life. She determined when I could sleep, when I could eat, when I could shower, clean my house, do my laundry, where and if I could go anyplace. Not only that, everything I did was done in a state of complete fatigue. About six weeks into this I looked around one day and knew that this was not the life I planned. And suddenly I desperately wanted out. Motherhood was not all it was cracked up to be. I wanted my old life back. I could not bear the thought of living the rest of my life out of control, in a completely fatigued state. In a flood of tears I dialed my mother.

"I've had it!" I cried to my mother. "I'm not cut out to be a mother! I can't do this the rest of my life. This child has taken over. I'm not even a person anymore. I want my old life back!"

She listened quietly as I unloaded for several tearful minutes. Then, quite unexpectedly, she started to laugh. "Well, guess what, dear," she said through her laughter. "It's too late!"

Her upbeat, jovial response disarmed me. I was completely taken back. She had managed with that simple, light quip to bring me back to earth. The fact that she found my tragic situation funny suddenly allowed me to step outside myself and see how pathetic I looked. It was a comical sight. And somehow her laughter let me know that she knew what this was like and that it wouldn't last forever.

On so many occasions since then, Mother's disarming humor has put things into perspective. She takes life seriously, but she doesn't take herself seriously.

What a gift!

CHAPTER EIGHT

A LISTENING
FRIEND

*

"HOW ARE YOU, REALLY?"

In Tokyo, 1962

One of the qualities of a true friend is the ability to listen, to communicate on a more meaningful plane than the superficial, "How are you?" level. When Marjorie Hinckley asks how you're doing, she really wants to know. One of her daughters-in-law explains:

When I was a young mother with four children ages four and under and a young busy bishop for a husband, Clark's parents would call every Sunday. I was always amazed at how they remembered the seemingly insignificant details of our life and asked the progress of each one of our projects with interest and concern. From spreading a truckload of dirt to getting our car repaired, they cared. But what I loved even more than the Sunday call was the phone call on Monday morning when Clark's mother would say, "Now, let's have some girl talk." She wanted to know how I was *really* doing and how I *really* felt about all that was going on in our busy lives. I could always expect that she would listen without judgment. She never interrupted with answers or anecdotes.

One time she said, "You must be climbing the walls with all those sick children, all these weeks, twenty-degree weather, and no family near." Whatever sense of discouragement or loneliness I might have felt fled at that moment of being understood. She didn't have Pollyanna answers or a set of instructions. She simply communicated that she knew how I felt. I could increase in capacity and stature, because I was understood. What a friend! Long before psychologists wrote books on "validation," she had a natural knack for listening with love and responding with understanding.

Maxine Grimm, who became a friend to Sister Hinckley in the early 1960s in the Philippines, says:

I particularly remember one luncheon when Marjorie and I ate alone in our home in Manila. Marjorie asked me many questions and I just unburdened myself of all my problems. In her sweet, quiet, and concerned way, she allayed all my fears, restored my faith, and put me back on track. What a tremendous relief to find peace through such a dear friend.

Barbara Smith, former General Relief Society President, speaks of Sister Hinckley's wonderful ability to be a friend—even to her own family members:

I appreciate an experience I had with Sister Marjorie Hinckley when she came with her family to the Far East. Given the opportunity to choose how she would like to celebrate her fiftieth wedding anniversary, she expressed a long-held desire to be together in the Orient with her five children and their spouses. Each family planned and saved, and her wish became a reality.

My husband, Douglas, was then serving as president of the Asia area of the Church. Although I had known Sister Hinckley before, watching her as she managed this group with her skillful but loving hand was to see her in a different perspective. She was mother, wife, mother-in-law, but first and always she was a friend to each person. The group seemed to grow closer with every excursion they took. In her humility and common touch with people, including her own family, I saw her give people a sense that if she feels they have worth, maybe they do.

I like to remember a scene in the Salt Lake Tabernacle the night of a general Relief Society meeting. President Hinckley was at the podium giving an address, and on the front row of the center section sat Sister Hinckley surrounded by daughters and granddaughters. Seeing her sitting there close to her girls and looking into the face of her husband as he spoke, to me pronounced her priorities— the things, the people that mattered the most to her. I felt that she was securing for time and beyond those relationships that are dearer than life yet are sometimes not given first place in our lives.

On yet another occasion, she was asked to speak at the fiftieth anniversary of the East Mill Creek Stake, in the area where they had lived for many years and where her husband had served as stake president. In her half-joking way she is reported to have said, "I hope you like me, because if you do not it is your fault. You've made me what I am." Not only is that charmingly put and effective but it also speaks some wisdom. It is the basis for thoughtful consideration we might all undertake about the influence we have as Church members on those around us in our wards. How do we treat one another? Do we include others, admire and praise them whenever we can to encourage goodness? Are we their friends?

When I saw the Hinckley family in faraway China, it didn't matter whether their relationship was a mother to child, in-law to in-law, or husband to wife, the happiness in that family came about because they were all friends. We do not need to travel as far as China to see that kind of love at work; it is a method meant for any who will believe in its power. I have found that it translates very well and it starts with trying.

Ruth Faust, wife of President James E. Faust, has observed and been a recipient of Sister Hinckley's wonderful powers of friendship.

I first became acquainted with Sister Marjorie P. Hinckley about forty years ago when our husbands were counselors to the stake presidents in neighboring stakes. Over the years I have watched her with great interest and admiration. I have learned much by observing her interactions with people. Whether it be a stranger, acquaintance, family member, or intimate friend, everyone is treated with great respect and sincere interest. She quickly finds a common thread for friendship, making everyone feel good after passing her way.

Through the years our paths have crossed more frequently, and I have treasured my association with her. Wives of the General Authorities have a great love and respect for Marjorie's openness and her common touch for making everyone feel comfortable around her. Her sense of humor is sometimes very disarming. Marjorie is always herself—very natural and sincere.

With children and their spouses in Hong Kong, 1987

Marjorie has so many qualities that I admire, such as warmth, friendship, and the common touch. She also possesses a wonderful mind of great capacity. She's the perfect example of how a woman in her position should be. I cannot overstate the influence for good Sister Hinckley has been on the many lives she has touched.

George H. Durham II recalls the friendship between the Hinckleys and his parents:

My sisters—Carolyn W. D. Person and Doralee D. Madsen—and I have had the special privilege of being witnesses to the life-long friendship between President Gordon B. Hinckley and our father, G. Homer Durham (1911–1985). One of the great dividends of that relationship was the friendship that developed between Sister Hinckley and our mother, Eudora Widtsoe Durham (1912–1995). Because of this friendship, Sister Hinckley accepted our invitation to speak at the funeral of our mother. She began by saying:

"Our friendship began years ago when she fell in love with Homer Durham, and I fell in love with Gordon Hinckley. These two young men were such fast friends that we knew that in order to endure it we would have to love each other. And how easy that came, like breathing in and breathing out."

Sister Hinckley's concluding words continue to comfort us as she testifies of friendship, love, the reality of the Resurrection, and of eternity:

"In the passing of Eudora I feel a void and a loneliness, for I have lost a friend. . . . Every conversation I have had with Eudora during the last few years ended the same way, by one of us saying: 'I love you,' and the other one saying 'I love you too.' These were not empty words, they were words of intense and deep feelings.

"There were many short separations in our lives as Homer and Eudora moved about during his illustrious career. But temporary separations had no effect on our close relationship. Distance means absolutely nothing. And so it is with this separation; our love for each other remains intact.

"So, I say again, as I have on so many other occasions: 'Good-bye, Eudora, I'll see you soon. I love you.'

"How grateful I am for the gospel and for the assurance that friendships are eternal."

Throughout her unique and remarkable life, Marjorie Pay Hinckley has represented many admirable things to many people, but to us she will always be our mother's friend.

Barbara Ballard, wife of Elder M. Russell Ballard of the Twelve, comments on Sister Hinckley as a friend:

Sister Hinckley is like a human magnet who draws people to her. Whenever she enters a room, she brightens it because of her cheery presence. She has such a caring way about her that she makes each individual feel as though she were a personal friend whom she would help in any way she could. This was very evident in my first close association with her. I was asked to serve on a committee with her shortly after my husband was called to be a General Authority. I was a bit overwhelmed by my assignment. Sister Hinckley was sensitive to my situation and feelings. She was tender and understanding and so helpful. I will always remember her for that.

Gerry Avant of the Church News staff describes her gratitude for the friendship and validation she has received from Sister Hinckley:

I've been acquainted with Sister Hinckley for about twenty-five years—ever since I started working at *Church News*—and have always been impressed with the concern and interest she has for me. In the mid-1970s, my father had a stroke that left him paralyzed and unable to speak. I worried constantly about him and traveled home to Georgia as often as I could to be with him and to help my mother, who had undertaken caring for him full-time. I don't remember when I told Sister Hinckley of my father's condition, but she never failed to inquire about him. "And how is your mother?" she would ask; she always expressed admiration for my mother's commitment to care for my father.

My father died in 1984. Since then, my mother has had problems with her health, especially during the past few years. I don't think there has been a single time that I've been in Sister Hinckley's presence that she has not asked, "How is your mother? Is everything okay with her?" Quite often she says, "Give your mother my love." Sister Hinckley acts as though she and my mother are longtime friends! That has given me so much comfort.

Rewarding though my job is, it sometimes becomes quite difficult and physically challenging. I've been sort of a pioneer—the first woman on the *Church News* staff to travel extensively on assignments. I've always felt that I've had to prove that I can do the job and do it as well as the men on the staff, so I've been extremely reluctant to admit that any task is too difficult, or to take time off to rest when I am tired or even sick while on assignments.

I get particularly tired hauling around camera equipment day in

121

and day out, toting it along with my carry-on bag to and from and through airports.

For some reason, it seems to make things easier when someone else acknowledges that I'm working hard and under difficult circumstances. From time to time, Sister Hinckley has commented on "that heavy camera bag." A few times, she has lifted it just to see how heavy it was and turned to others saying, "Feel how heavy that bag is. She carries that thing all over the place!" After such "fussing over," it has seemed much easier to pick up the bag and carry on.

Colleen Maxwell, wife of Elder Neal A. Maxwell of the Twelve, remembers:

I learned a sweet lesson from Sister Hinckley when she went out of her way to encourage a sister who had experienced a difficult family stigma along with disapproval from many. I watched Sister Hinckley as she befriended this sister and took her under her wing. All who saw her love and concern were touched by her example.

Sister Hinckley always seems to understand how people feel, whether they are family members or brand-new acquaintances. In 1996, the Riverton Wyoming Stake held dedicatory services for monuments built to remember the tragedy of the handcart companies in the winter of 1856. There was more than one monument and more than one meeting and certainly more than one speech. Katrina Glenn (age ten) hadn't met Sister Hinckley before that day, but when asked what the best part of the day was, she said:

The best experience that day was when Sister Hinckley held my hand for one whole minute. She said to me, "After all those meetings you have come here to listen to another one. Do you think you can make it?"

Laura Willes, a niece, describes one particular trait that she loves about Aunt Marge:

We all appreciate her well-developed ability to pay attention to the individual and to listen from the heart. When she looks you in the eye and says "How are you?" she really wants to know and listens with keen attention, sympathy, and understanding. It is always satisfying to be singled out by Aunt Marge because you know that she really cares and is interested in everything you have to tell her.

Kathleen H. Barnes, a daughter, relates a childhood memory of her mother's loving attention to and interest in individuals:

Brother Stange was our ward custodian. He lived in a little house near the church. He was a German immigrant, and his thick accent and strong opinions greatly intimidated me. The church was his castle, and he took great ownership and pride in it. This could be frightening for a child who might have dropped a gum wrapper in the hall or been found running down the ramp toward the basement classrooms. You didn't want him to open your classroom door and see you tilting back on your chair! He was not the least bit shy about lecturing you on your responsibility to keep the ward house clean and in good repair.

You didn't want to run into Brother Stange on Saturday night after the ward show. Popcorn on the cultural hall floor was not exactly his idea of preparing the building for the Sabbath. It always seemed to me that he was a child's worst enemy.

I guess that is why I could never figure out why Mother liked him. Each week after Primary she would take me by the hand and we would walk across the church grounds to visit Brother Stange. The protection of her presence allowed me the chance to see

Brother Stange as a person. We would often find him sitting at his table eating raw hamburger filled with chopped onions—a dish he learned to like in the "old country." In fact, Mother would sometimes make a special trip to the butcher to buy high-quality ground beef for this man. There, in his own home, Brother Stange's demeanor was kind and humble and he always thanked us for our visit.

As we walked home, Mother would express appreciation for this "good man" and lament that he was without the companionship of family and had few friends.

Mother has an ability to see beyond the exterior and look into people's hearts.

Phyllis Duncan, a childhood friend, describes Marjorie's early intuitive gift for friendship:

When Marge and I were about ten or eleven years old, it became the "in" thing that Christmastime to have a brown wool skirt and a red rouge-neck (pullover) sweater, to be topped with a wide-brimmed brown beaver hat. Wanting to be right up with the styles, Marge and I ordered said outfits as our main Christmas gift from Santa. And of course, we both were very thrilled to see them on Christmas morning.

Well, during the Christmas week we decided to go downtown to a movie. In those days it was safe and common for us to ride the streetcar into town, which we planned to do. When Marge came out to meet me, we were both very excited about how terrific we were decked out—except for one thing. Marge was carrying a lovely pair of brown kid gloves, and hurried to explain that her Aunt Francis, who was her mother's

Marjorie (center) and friends, 1929

124

sister, and who had a good job and liked to give Marge nice things, had given her this very attractive pair of gloves to go with her outfit. Marge was afraid this might keep us from looking just alike. Very quickly it occurred to her that she should give me one and she would keep one and we each would carry a glove. This seemed a perfect solution, so on we went to catch the bus.

I can still see the amused faces of the other bus riders as they watched Marge and me happily enter the bus in all of our glory, sporting our beautiful new outfits, complete with one glove each.

As I remember, we never again appeared in matching clothes until all five of us girls from the First Ward had matching black-and-white-checked jackets in high school, which was the "in" thing to do at *that* time.

Then, several decades later, it happened again! I was the ward Relief Society president and had asked Marge to come and speak to my Relief Society. Wanting to look particularly nice for the day, I purchased a brown suit. When Marge came into the room, all eyes turned toward her. We were wearing identical suits! Everyone smiled and we broke into laughter. Marge did nothing until she arose to speak, and then warmly told about how as girls growing up we wanted to have everything alike—the same color, the same style, everything. She pointed out that to see that we had chosen to wear the same outfits that day only made her remember the good times and close friendship of those long-ago years. She succeeded in making what might have been a tense moment into a time for sharing happy memories and strengthening a friendship.

A niece, Beth Lloyd Stettler, tells of a time Aunt Marge gave loving support and a listening ear:

Several years ago our fourth child was born. We were so thrilled to have another healthy baby. A few hours after he was born, the doctors told us that he had a heart defect and was in critical condition. A Life-Flight helicopter was on the way to transport him to Primary Children's Medical Center. This would be the first of several stays at the hospital.

Michael had open-heart surgery on the day that he turned two months old. The normal hospital stay for such a procedure is ten days; Michael exceeded that by about two weeks. It seemed that if something could go wrong, it would with Michael.

This was a very trying time for our young family. Our faith was constantly being tested. We relied heavily on the support of friends and family.

Aunt Marge was one of our greatest supporters. I would receive phone calls from her almost daily during our stay at the hospital. I looked forward to the calls. She gave me the encouragement I needed to face another day of not knowing what would happen next. She listened, and she always seemed to say the things that I needed to hear the most on that particular day. Every call she made would give me the courage to face another day of extreme emotional and spiritual challenges. Even though the calls seldom lasted more than five minutes, they always left me feeling better, renewed my hope, and strengthened my faith. I knew that I could face another problem and go on and be just fine.

Aunt Marge's loving support and listening ear made a very difficult time in my life much easier.

Peggy H. Andersen served with her husband in the Northern Far East Mission during the time when Elder Hinckley supervised the area. She was with Sister Hinckley in numerous missionary report meetings, testimony

meetings, district conferences, and servicemen's groups, as well as infor-
mal conversations. She says of Sister Hinckley:

She is undoubtedly the *best listener* in the whole Church. She
never seems to tire of what one has to say, and often asks more questions to keep one going. People were never intimidated by her;
rather they were drawn in by her kindness and the interest she
showed in them. If anyone needed encouragement, Sister Hinckley
was the answer. Missionaries would flock around her just to shake
her hand, to have a chance to sit down by her and listen to her
humor, or to pour out their hearts to her. I wrote
in my journal: "I feel so much better after spending time with Sister Hinckley yesterday."

Rhee Ho Nam, an early member of the Church in
Korea, was the beneficiary of Sister Hinckley's atten-
tion to and interest in individuals.

Sister Hinckley often accompanied Elder
Gordon B. Hinckley to Korea, the "Land of the
Morning Calm," during the early sixties. The Church's place in
Korea was in its infancy and beset by many difficulties, both inher-
ited and unforeseen. On a national level, the aftermath and the
memories of the Korean War were not necessarily explained or
comforted away; spiritually, the few of us baptized members in the
Church were challenged by inexperience.

President and Sister Hinckley did not simply visit the Saints of
Korea. They got to know us and our personal struggles.

One of my unforgettable memories was a conference with
President and Sister Hinckley. After the meeting Sister Hinckley
turned to me and pointed out one of the sisters chatting some

With Inez Hunter, wife of President Howard W. Hunter, 1998 distance away. She asked, with a particularly keen interest, the name of this young woman. I readily replied, "Oh, her name is Youn Soon Park." The readiness of my response was by no means mechanical or formal. I had already noticed Youn Soon in testimony meetings and other church meetings. It was hard not to notice her, not simply for her exquisite beauty, but also for her exemplary and steadfast testimony of the gospel.

Then, to my pleasant surprise, Sister Hinckley went on to confirm and encourage my admiration for Youn Soon. She said, "Youn Soon has a beautiful testimony and never fails to be at a meeting." Her gentle but peculiarly firm observation sealed up my shy streak, and I felt as though I had a thumbs-up from above.

I eventually married this beautiful sister. As I look back at that day now, I see how Sister Hinckley's expressions of real interest in me made a difference.

A nephew, Bryant Wadsworth, tells his story of "How are you, really?"

I went into the mission field an idealist. I thought I knew a lot about missionary work. But in early September 1962, when I arrived in Kyoto, Japan, I realized that day-to-day missionary work was nothing like I thought it would be.

It was hot and muggy. I could not understand the language. And most discouraging of all, missionaries were still mortal beings with jealousies and faults like everyone else.

I was homesick. I struggled along with this kind of discouragement for nearly three months. My only solace was the early morning hours when I was awake alone and could pour out my heart to the Lord in prayer.

Then Elder and Sister Hinckley arrived in the mission. I was thrilled to see Uncle Gordon and Aunt Marge, but it was a little awkward. I didn't want to be conspicuous in my delight and I wasn't sure it would be proper to even hint to those around me that they were more than "visiting authorities" to me. Still, I badly needed private time with them.

The first meeting, which began at 8:00 A.M., lasted until we broke for lunch at 1:00 P.M. Elder Hinckley did some personal interviews during the lunch break, and then we reconvened while he instructed us. He then returned to personal interviews.

I went up to greet Aunt Marge, hoping to get a minute alone with her. She took me aside, and we searched for a place where we could be out of the way and have some privacy. We sat down in the kitchen. She asked me how I was doing. Soon I was dumping into her welcoming lap all of my anxieties, discouragements, and troubles. She listened with sympathy and understanding. We would talk for a minute, and then I would cry for a while and she would cry with me. Then we would laugh because most of the worst of my hard experiences seemed to be over—something I hadn't fully realized until this talk.

I shall never forget how kind and considerate she was. At one point she assured me I would be okay because, she said, "You have faith." This really helped me. I felt if she believed that, then it must be true.

We were occasionally interrupted by someone needing a drink of water or wanting to use the phone. Normally this would have added to my anxiety, but for some reason it didn't bother me at all. I went right on talking, bawling, and laughing. We must have been together for an hour or more.

Time for my interview came. I sat down in the chair across the desk from Elder Hinckley and said, "I have just unloaded all my troubles and thoughts on Aunt Marge. She will tell them to you. I don't need to take the time to repeat them here." We talked about things in general, my health, my self-control, my impressions of Japan, the language and its difficulty, and so on. He encouraged me and then asked if I had any questions. Hesitantly, I asked for a priesthood blessing. The blessing that followed has been a significant guide in my life since that day. I think I would not have been in the right frame of mind to receive this blessing if it hadn't been for the wonderful help I had just received from Aunt Marge.

I came away from this experience a new man. It was the turning point in my mission and in many ways the turning point in my life. Only my own mother could have helped me as Sister Hinckley did.

The typical greeting Marjorie Hinckley gives sincerely to literally thousands of people is: "Hello, my friend." In those three words lie enough acceptance and love to get you through any day. And as she looks you in the eyes, you might find yourself unburdening how you really are!

CONFIDENCE
BUILDER

*

"I JUST DON'T KNOW HOW YOU DO IT ALL! YOU'RE AMAZING"

With parents and siblings, 1960. Standing, from left, Marjorie, Helen Elizabeth, Joanne, Douglas, Dorene, and Evelyn. Seated, Georgetta and Phillip LeRoy Pay

Marjorie Hinckley has an amazing way of inspiring confidence in every encounter. To her each person is a constant source of wonder and awe—continually the object of her spontaneous exclamations: "I can't believe how smart you are. I can't believe how good you are! I can't believe that you can really do that! Aren't you something!" These phrases are so simple, but so completely sincere—without guile, and certainly devoid of any attempt to manipulate. They aren't even meant to manipulate you into being better. But better is what you want to be. Universally, every person walks away standing a little taller and thinking: "Maybe she's right. I must be a pretty good person—definitely above average—and it's amazing how many things I can do. In fact, I think I'll go do some more good things!"

Virginia H. Pearce, a daughter, describes her mother's encouraging words:

In 1993, as a member of the Young Women General Presidency, I was assigned to speak in general conference. It would be a great understatement to say that preparing a talk for that setting is intimidating. It is, in fact, downright terrifying. Whatever confidence I ever had immediately vaporized when I read the letter of assignment. After weeks of prayer and work, the day approached. Sometime between finishing the talk and giving it to the TelePrompTer people, I gave a copy of it to my mother. That evening she called. "You're amazing. This talk is so wonderful. I can't believe you can do all that you do." I listened like a thirsty traveler in the desert. She went on to describe parts she liked. "I especially like the story about the little boy and the dart game," she said.

After I hung up the phone, I stood a little taller. Shook a little less. Maybe I would be able to speak in the Tabernacle after all. Mother definitely thought I could. And then I thought about the story she had referred to:

A mother was busily preparing dinner when her little boy burst into the kitchen. "Mother, will you play darts with me?" "Just-a-minutes" didn't seem to satisfy the little boy, so the mother followed him down the basement stairs. As they came into the playroom, she said, "I don't know the rules or how to play."

"Oh, it's not hard at all," he beamed confidently. "I just stand right here and throw the darts, and you stand over there and say, 'Wonderful! Wonderful!'"

Without realizing it, I had repeated a story that described my own mother perfectly!

A son-in-law, Alan Barnes, describes a similar conversation that had the identical effect:

It was a short time after taking a new job that we found ourselves at a dinner engagement with some friends and my mother-in-law. During the course of the conversation, a friend asked how I had secured this new position. I gave credit to a mutual friend who had introduced me to the position and had subsequently spoken in my behalf. I suggested that it was because of him and his kindness that I had been selected.

My mother-in-law listened to this exchange and at the conclusion she leaned across the table and put her hand on my arm. "Now," she said, "let me tell you the real story. He got that job because he was the most qualified candidate!"

True or not, it mattered little. What mattered was that in that instant she validated my worth. She believed in me! Since that occasion I have been filled with a great desire never to disappoint her. That same trust and belief in me has been reaffirmed time and time again. Through the years she has restated it in a number of ways.

I shall always be grateful for her support.

One son, Clark, describes his mother's absolute confidence in her children—sometimes completely ill-founded!

Early in the fall of seventh grade, during that brave new world of junior high, I had a science class assignment to make an insect collection. Although we were given several weeks' notice, I characteristically waited until the last few days to begin collecting my insects. As a result, I had a couple of very busy nights trapping bugs around the porch light and mounting them—not too neatly—on a piece of foamcore board. When the project grades came out, I received a well-deserved "C" on my collection.

Mother was incensed—not with me, but with a teacher who, in her mind, didn't know an "A" project when he saw one. Mother, of course, had seen only my last-minute flurry of activity stretching into a late-night vigil around the porch light, not the large and neatly mounted collections of other students.

I knew the real story, of course. I had received a "C" because I had turned in "C" work. I also knew that to protect the reputation of an innocent teacher, I had better get started earlier next time and do the "A" work that Mother assumed I was doing.

A daughter-in-law remembers:

A few years ago I was discussing with my mother-in-law one of the decisions facing my daughter. Her observation was, "She will not make a mistake in a matter of this importance." I was able to rely on her confidence as I watched my daughter work through the problem and discover the answers for herself. She does not try to direct the outcome or interfere. She sincerely believes each one of us has the wherewithal to do the right thing, and she communicates that belief. Her confidence empowers others to make the right choices.

Rosemary P. Olsen, a granddaughter, expresses similar feelings:

My grandmother calls me from time to time to see how we are doing. It always brightens my day. She is a great confidence builder, and after a conversation with her I always come away standing a little taller. She makes me feel like I can conquer the world. She has the ability to see the strengths in a person and acknowledge and encourage them.

A sister, Evelyn, has early memories of the heightened sense of confidence Sister Hinckley gives in every encounter:

My sister Marjorie is seven years older than the next child in our family. Consequently, she was the first married, and all five of us younger ones were enamored with this young couple. A narrow dirt lane led up to the first little cottage where Marjorie and Gordon lived in the country. It was five miles from our house, and mostly uphill. However, we girls at home shared a bicycle, and it was great exercise to cycle those miles. It was worth it to be able to visit Marjorie and to sometimes help her clean her house so it would be ready for entertaining guests. In fact, she had me convinced that it would be impossible for her to have a party without my or one of my sisters' help.

Their living room was lined on three walls with waist-high bookcases and windows directly above them. It was sunny and cheerful. Obviously, they loved to read. As we dusted the books and worked together, Marjorie and I did a lot of talking and laughing. The conversations seemed to go like this:

"Have you read *Anne of Green Gables* yet, Evelyn?"

"Oh, yes. And I loved it."

"Be sure you get the sequels, because they're just as good."

"I love it when there's more to the story," I added.

"It really pleases me that you are such a good reader, Evelyn. Reading is really fun, isn't it! Tell me about school," she asked. "And tell me all about the family."

I knew that she talked by phone to Mother every day, so I was pleased that she still wanted to hear all these things from me. She wanted to know about everything I was doing and how I felt about everything. She was interested in all my friends and all the family.

Looking back, I realize she used this time for teaching moments also. She probably learned this from Mother. "Temple marriage is so wonderful, Evelyn," she would say. "I still have the priesthood in my home, just like you have it with Daddy."

Before I realized it, we had the cleaning done. We relaxed on the swing and sipped refreshing lemonade. She convinced me that I was *the* best: the most well-trained, the most skilled, the most cheerful, the most excellent, the most indispensable helper. I believed her!

As I rode my bike home, which was thankfully all downhill now, I was contented and happy, feeling good about myself and my sister.

When I was promoted from junior high, my girlfriends and I wanted to celebrate. I suggested we hike out to Marjorie's home. They liked the idea. We each found a long stick, wrapped our lunch in a large bandanna, and tied it to the end of the stick. With the sticks over our shoulders, we hiked the five miles out of the city and through the farmland. Marjorie welcomed us with her usual sisterly hospitality.

"I can't believe that with all the things to choose from, you all chose to come out here. It really makes me happy and I feel very special!" she exclaimed.

She insisted on getting the old horse out for us so we could take turns riding around the yard. This was a treat for us "city" girls. Of course, she made lemonade, and we stretched out on the shady lawn and felt as though we were in a classy resort.

Sixty years later, my sisters and brother and I meet weekly at Marjorie's apartment. She greets us with the same delight she did so long ago: "With all you have to do, I can't believe you came. You are so wonderful!"

And the fact is that by the time we leave to "pedal" back to our homes, we really believe that we are somewhat wonderful! She's pretty convincing.

Clark Hinckley, a son, remembers one act of encouragement that had a long-term effect:

When I was applying to graduate schools, I had carefully selected a couple of top programs as well as a couple of less competitive programs where I had a better chance of being accepted. One day as I was preparing the admission forms, Mother said, "Why don't you apply to Harvard?" My answer was simple—there was no sense wasting several hours and the $50 application fee to apply to a school where I clearly did not have the qualifications to be accepted. But Mother, whose opinion of her children's abilities always exceeded our own, simply said, "I'll pay the $50 if you'll complete the application."

This turned out to be one of those little conversations that changed my life forever. It was as a student at Harvard that I met my future wife.

Sister Hinckley used her many talents to support her children and boost their confidence in themselves. A daughter describes how her mother's help always seemed to empower rather than overwhelm. It was a leg up, not a demonstration of superiority.

Mother has always had a certain amount of creative energy. On so many occasions I was the recipient of it. When I was just five years old, Dad was working for the Denver and Rio Grande Railroad as part of the war effort, and we were transferred to Denver.

As Easter approached, I was assigned to give an Easter poem in

Junior Sunday School. Because we had rented a furnished home, and had moved nothing but our personal items, we had no books or magazines that contained anything suitable for a child to learn. In addition, Mother did not have a car, so there was no way to get to a public library. Typically, she took matters into her own hands and sat down and wrote a poem:

> Some folks think that Easter time is just for fancy clothes,
> For Easter eggs and baskets and colored straw galore.
> But Mother told me differently,
> She says it's much, much more.
> It means that Jesus died
> So we could live forevermore.

When I was in junior high, I was taking a speech class in which one assignment was to give a five-minute presentation in front of the class. The subject was unassigned, but our task was to capture the attention of our audience and sustain that attention for five minutes.

I was a timid child, and the thought of standing before my peers for five minutes was bad enough, but to have to keep their attention was more than I could bear to think about. Mother reassured me and suggested that the best way to keep people's attention is to talk about them by name. So we devised an elaborate story about a dream. In this dream I saw the students in the class. I then began to mention each one by name, telling something about them.

Mother's idea was a resounding success.

Through years of dancing, she encouraged me, often helping me create dance ideas. She taught me to see things in a creative way.

As a senior in high school, I had to write the script for a school assembly. Once again, I brought my task home to Mother, and together we sat at the kitchen table and brainstormed. Out of her creative mind came an idea, and my assembly was born.

Time and time again, she sat with me and stimulated my thinking. She was the spark behind high school campaigns, seminary devotionals, two-and-a-half-minute talks, English papers, and dozens of other assignments. She reaffirmed my timid desires. She encouraged creative thinking, and I always came away feeling that my ideas were noteworthy.

Elder Bruce Hafen of the Seventy speaks of this unique quality of helping without taking over:

The best thing about Sister Hinckley's approach to helping others is the confidence she gives them in themselves. She doesn't come to help with the attitude that only she can save you; rather, she comes to uplift you, and somehow leaves you honestly believing you're so good you hardly need her help.

This contagious belief in the goodness of others bespeaks the gentle yet somehow stirring leadership of both Sister Hinckley and her husband. Together, they reflect an old Chinese proverb: "A leader is best when people barely know he exists. . . . Of a good leader, who talks little, when his work is done and his aim fulfilled, they will say, 'We did it ourselves.'"

Another daughter gives her own example of her mother's constant support and confidence-building ways.

One day Mother, my sister, and I were chatting casually. We shared a great love for children's literature, and my sister and I were bemoaning the dearth of Church books for children. Writing children's books was something I had always wanted to do, and Mother spoke right up: "Why don't you two write some yourself? I'll take your children to the park (four under age four, not counting the two babies) one day next week so that you can do it." Well, how could we pass up such an offer! A whole day free, and with our mother's confidence so sure. The day came. She took the children. We worked on a book. Of course, it took more than one work period, but after that first day we were committed and we could collaborate with countless children underfoot. Over the next few years we wrote and found a friendly publisher for several books.

We look back at our incredible naiveté, to think that we—a couple of unpublished mothers in their twenties—would have the temerity to think that we could write books that someone would buy! But we did, and they did. The whole adventure was a response to our needs as mothers, our dreams, a timely offer for a day of baby-sitting, and most of all to a mother's matter-of-fact confidence in her daughters.

Michael Hinckley, a grandson, relates how his grandmother always makes him feel good about himself:

My grandparents are always happy to have me drop by for a visit. Whenever I speak of problems or disappointments, they both encourage me and assure me that "everything will work out." They tell me they are proud of me, and I always come away feeling great.

Recently I was telling my grandparents that I had reconsidered what I wanted to do for a career and was thinking about going into medicine. I said that this would mean a lot of extra schooling, and I wouldn't be able to start practicing medicine until I was about thirty-six years old. Grandma quickly replied, "You'll be thirty-six when you're thirty-six anyway—even if you don't change careers!"

Putting things into perspective and giving you confidence in yourself is one of Grandma's gifts. She gives people the desire to be good and to improve their lives. She'll always be one of my heroes.

A daughter-in-law, Jane F. Hinckley, remembers her mother-in-law's confidence-building affirmations:

I must admit I fell in love with my future mother-in-law almost before I fell in love with her son Richard. I always knew that she would be the best mother-in-law a person could ever have. No one could have been better. She has never corrected me. She has never criticized me. She has always been so accepting.

One Sunday evening, early in our marriage, we were visiting Dick's parents. His mother wasn't feeling well and was lying down. We offered to fix dinner for the family. I peeled and mashed some red potatoes. After we served them to everyone, Dick said, "I don't think you're supposed to mash red potatoes." His mother quickly said, "Jane can mash any kind of potatoes she wants to mash! They're delicious."

That was typical. I have never felt judged. She has always expressed confidence in me and admiration for everything I do.

This kind of constant building of others has the magical effect of immediately making you want to do better. In essence, planting the desire to be better is the best thing a true teacher can do. In a talk to young people, Sister Hinckley reflected back on just such a teacher from her past:

I wish I could make you feel the way a Sunday School teacher made me feel one Sunday morning when I was about fifteen. I remember leaving his class and during the walk home

Marjorie (center) with aunt and grandmother

thinking, "I am going to be very good. I am going to be the best person I know how to be." What a wonderful teacher he was.

Her wish is a reality. She is a teacher who does make everyone want to be a little better. In formal and informal teaching situations, she delivers the expectations couched in language of respect and confidence in the learners' motivations and abilities. Put-downs or humiliation are never part of the teaching moment.

One daughter relates a conversation when a reprimand or warning came in a package that looked like a compliment.

When my future husband and I were dating—I believe engaged at the time—Mother said to me one morning, following a very late night: "You're so lucky. Jim is such an affectionate person and he'll be a great husband. But that affection is something you're going to have to be careful about now." That's all she said. She didn't indicate that she needed a response from me.

I was a little startled—sexual morality was an area I had not heard her venture into before—but the warning was not lost on me. She casually wrapped it in a warm blanket of support and generous feelings toward both of us. Those few short sentences left me feeling approved of, proud of my choice of a husband, and in control of the current situation. Her warning was easy to hear and helped shape my behavior.

A son reflects on his mother's great ability to seize the teaching moment.

I once read that good parenting is largely the art of becoming a supreme opportunist—seizing those unexpected and unanticipated teaching opportunities. I distinctly remember being on the student end of one such moment. As a young boy I teasingly referred to one of my siblings as a fool. It was said in a jokingly complimentary way, not meant as an insult, but the word *fool* was a word Mother didn't like. She instantly invited me into the living room where she sat me down, handed me a Bible, and asked me to open it to Matthew 5:22 and read the verse aloud. I have never forgotten the last phrase: "Whosoever shall say, Thou fool, shall be in danger of hell fire." It was a powerful lesson!

Sarah Dudley, a granddaughter, recalls:

Throughout my life, Grandma has been a wonderful teacher, because she always teaches by expressing confidence in me and by her example. I remember when my family and I were visiting her and Grandpa one Sunday. I asked if I could help her do her dishes. She replied, "No, Sarah. That can wait until Monday. Today let's just rest and give thanks." She probably doesn't recall that, but it has stuck in my mind. She is a wonderful grandma and is still teaching me a great deal about life.

Teaching without humiliating. Expressing confidence by what she doesn't say as well as by what she does say. Even the neighborhood children benefited from Sister Hinckley's effective communication style, as her son's friend Russell T. Osguthorpe remembers:

Sister Hinckley was clear in her communication with Clark and me, but never harsh. I knew she had faith and confidence in us as children, even when we had done something wrong.

When I was about twelve years old, I was playing in the park with Clark when his mother gave him her keys and asked if he would get something out of the car for her. On our way to the parking lot, I matter-of-factly said, "I know how to drive your car."

"You do not," Clark challenged.

"Oh yes I do," I said. "Just give me the keys, and I'll show you."

He gave me the keys, and we jumped in the car. I started it, pulled it out of the parking place, drove it down to the end of the parking lot, turned it around, and headed back to re-park it. Cars were positioned on both sides of the space we were entering, and I almost missed both of them. Just as I was braking, we heard that scraping noise that any driver—even one as inexperienced as I—recognizes immediately. Our right rear fender had grazed the bumper of the car in the next space. My first inclination was to find somewhere to hide, but we both got out of the car, examined the dent in the fender, and noted that there had been no damage done to the other car.

We locked the car and returned with the items Sister Hinckley had requested. Even though she was one of the kindest people I have ever known, I couldn't muster the courage to say anything as we approached her. Looking at the ground, Clark finally muttered, "We dented the car."

"What do you mean, you dented the car?" she replied.

"We drove it," Clark said.

Looking back at her son and somewhat forgetting that I was there, Sister Hinckley gasped, "Whatever gave you the idea that you could drive a car?"

At this point, things had gone far enough. I couldn't stand there any longer and let my friend take the blame for what I had done.

"Clark didn't drive it, I did," I told her.

With the same shock that she had evidenced when she thought her son was the driver, she asked me the same question she'd asked Clark. I told her that I was sorry, and she immediately accepted my apology. I can't remember anything else about the picnic that day, except that I had a sick feeling in the pit of my stomach just thinking about what I'd done: I had dented my neighbor's car, and I didn't have any money to repair it.

That evening when we sat down to dinner, everyone was uncharacteristically quiet. Dad, who could be quite stern at times, finally looked at me and said, "I understand that you had a problem today." Apparently, he had already talked with Sister Hinckley, and they had examined the dent together. I could hardly believe that my dad was not upset with me, but he had no anger at all in his voice. He continued, "Do you think you can earn the money it will take to fix the dent?" I assured him that I would do anything to pay for it. He looked back as if he understood just how miserable I felt, and said, "I will get the car fixed, and then you can pay me back."

The car was repaired, I earned the money to reimburse my dad, and I never heard another word about the incident. Sister Hinckley never mentioned it to me, and neither did any of her children. I don't know if it was even discussed at their dinner table. They all allowed me to keep my dignity and self-confidence.

A daughter talks about her mother's willingness to teach without insisting that a person learn!

In all of Mother's relationships, there is an easy unconditionality. If you wipe the drainboards off in a different direction than she does, do your laundry differently, or approach a Relief Society lesson your own way, she expresses wonder and delight rather than making it a point to "help you do it right" the next time. Always words of admiration and validation. Never critical judgments. The net result: No one has to "perform." People can use all of their energy to get on with the business of living. Maybe this is what they call "unconditional love."

After I became an adult, I don't remember her ever telling me how I should or should not do things, being critical, or even giving advice. But I do remember one time when she offered a suggestion.

Unlike women of character, I have always been able to sleep quite comfortably at night with dirty dinner dishes all over the kitchen. After I've fixed and served dinner, I have just enough energy rationed out to do the "getting-the-kids-to-bed" routine. Barely. However, I have boundless morning energy, and I quite like whipping the kitchen into shape first thing.

Mother came to help me when my twins were born. After observing my habit of leaving the kitchen cluttered at night, as well as my inability to get a handle on the other housework, laundry, child care, and so on, she said: "Ginny, you might be better off if you just did the dishes at night. Then you could start every day with at least a clean kitchen." So unlike her was the comment that I remember exactly where both of us were standing when she made it. But, as unusual as it was, her voice still said that it was entirely my option. I didn't take the advice, and I don't believe she ever mentioned it again. It really shows your mettle as a teacher when you can offer an idea and then let go. And I don't think she was even biting her tongue.

A neighbor, Douglas E. Bagley, remembers Sister Hinckley as a teacher:

When I was growing up, the Hinckleys lived on the east side of 2700 East, while our family lived on the west side. I remember being in either a Primary class or a Sunday School class where Sister Hinckley gave the lesson. She doesn't remember that she was ever a regular teacher of mine, but I can remember her demeanor during the class. She was well prepared. We were a normal, energetic class. Nonetheless, her kindness and intelligence carried our interest for the duration of class time. She must have been a substitute, as I can remember thinking how wonderful it would be to be in her class permanently!

Ramona Hinckley Sullivan, a sister-in-law, remembers Marjorie as a wonderful teacher long before she was married:

When we were all growing up in the First Ward of Liberty Stake, we lived directly across the street from Marjorie Pay's family on Seventh South. There were no television sets, very few automobiles, some recreational activities, but for the most part we had to create our own entertainment. We would gather together five or six of our close neighborhood friends and try to think of something to do.

My group was several years younger than Marge's group. On one occasion we asked the older girls—or someone else had prevailed upon them—to teach us a few things about what to wear and how to improve ourselves. They proceeded to do just that.

We were silly, giggling eight- or nine-year-olds trying to be serious so that these older girls could pass on all their wisdom. It took time and patience—all day. We all persevered. It was worth the effort: even though we were not perfect, we had improved. We worked with our hair, brushing and styling it. We cleaned our shoes. We were told that if we would hang our clothes on hangers in the closet, they would always be ready for the next wearing. It was really fun. Last but not least, Marge told us to smile. A smile would cover up mistakes, add pleasure and happiness to our day, and help hide our embarrassment and self-consciousness when needed.

Mostly, it was always available, and you always had it with you. I've never forgotten those wise words from a great teacher.

Joan Hinckley Willes Peterson, a niece, describes her aunt's confidence-inspiring teaching techniques:

It has been forty-seven years since Aunt Marge taught me to tie "the bow," but it seems only a moment ago in my clear recollection.

"Sleeping over" was practically unheard of in the 1950s. It was a very special treat, at least in my neighborhood. I enjoyed just two sleepovers during my growing-up years, so every detail is vividly imprinted.

My mother, Ruth Hinckley Willes, gathered her children together one summer morning and we left our home on the avenues of Salt Lake City for a trip to "the farm." The roads, speed limits, and

my mother's slow driving made the travel to East Mill Creek feel like a hundred-mile jaunt. In reality it is but a twenty-minute drive nowadays.

After a wonderful day of family fun, Aunt Marge suggested to Mother that I might like to sleep over! Mother said yes, and I was in heaven. The gray Ford left without me, and I spent the rest of the day and evening playing every childhood game we could think of and watching almost-four-year-old Clark walk on broken glass with his toughened, country feet. I was stung by a bee and kissed by the sun; I giggled until my sides hurt and bathed by donning one of Kathy's bathing suits and having a water fight.

The next morning found Aunt Marge at the kitchen sink fixing

148

breakfast, her family bustling around her. She was always genuinely happy to have her children underfoot, and that included me, for the moment. I had arrived in an old skirt and blouse, played in them, and put them on again the next morning. It seems strange to me now in this casual era of wearing pants for almost everything, but back then girls often wore old skirts or dresses to play in, and we were not allowed to wear pants to school.

The skirt was full, with a ruffle along the bottom and a four-inch-wide sash that began at each side seam and tied in the back in a large bow. I had tried for years to make a bow that went across my waist, beautiful and flat, with tails hanging straight down. Each time, as I twisted around to view my work in the mirror, I found it kitty-corner, reaching for my shoulder blade. I would pull and fluff, but to no avail. My father had taught me how to tie my shoes as I sat on the front step one day when I was four, and that was the scope of my bow lessons.

Dear Aunt Marge asked me if I would like to have her tie my long sash for me, and I said yes. She dried her hands, sat down in the chair behind me, as if this were the most important event of her day, and tied the most beautiful bow I had ever seen. It was perfect! The loops faced straight across my waist on either side, with the material pulled out smoothly so the full four inches showed and the tails hung straight down.

"How did you do that, Aunt Marge? I love it!" I exclaimed. Then I had the bow lesson that changed my tying forever. "First, tie the sash once as you always do," she said. "Then see which sash is coming out on top and which one is coming out underneath. Make the bow loop in the underneath sash, and then bring the top sash straight down across the base of the loop and through; then pull it tight. Smooth it out and you're done. The important thing is to always bring the top one straight down, around, and through."

I thanked her and practiced, first on my shoe and then on my sash. In five minutes I was an expert, and I loved it. And oh, I loved Aunt Marge.

I have tied perfect bows on my darling daughters' dresses and the ponytails of tiny granddaughters, but the last bow of great significance, I tied with Aunt Marge standing beside me. It was for my dear mother, lying in her coffin. The bow was perfect, just as Aunt Marge had taught me so long ago when she took a moment to move a young child forward.

Janet Lee, wife of the late Rex E. Lee, remembers:

During my husband's tenure as president of BYU, I had many occasions to be taught by Sister Hinckley's gentle spirit. Each time I was with her, I left feeling uplifted, encouraged, and desirous of being a better person. Usually our conversations were brief. They took place while we were waiting for a devotional to begin, attending graduation while our husbands took their places on the stand, or seated together at a dinner. Each interaction was a learning experience for me, and I grew to look forward to our meetings with joyful anticipation.

At graduation one April, Sister Hinckley and I were seated long before the processional began. I was especially excited to be there because one of our daughters was graduating. We began talking about the joy of watching children grow up and make good choices. I mentioned how busy life had been for us with the responsibilities of BYU. I shared my concern that my younger children were growing up fast and I wanted to spend as much time with them as possible, despite my busy schedule. She talked about her children, grandchildren, and great-grandchildren. I knew how full her life had always been, combining a big family with the responsibilities that came to her because of her husband's various positions. I think I expected her to tell me how important it is to do it all. She said simply, "Family is everything."

I already knew how much I valued my family, but even now when I get caught up in the rush and responsibilities of life, I remind myself, "Family is everything."

Patricia Holland, wife of Elder Jeffrey R. Holland of the Twelve, refers to Sister Hinckley's gifted way of building confidence in every encounter— sometimes with words, sometimes with a note, or sometimes with just the squeeze of a hand.

When it comes to Marjorie Pay Hinckley, I do not wish to speak of her nearly so much as I wish to hug and kiss and squeeze her. Setting aside the love of members of my own family, Sister Hinckley has probably done as much to bless and cheer and encourage me these past years as any other woman in my life. At crucial times or in moments of need, during difficult challenges or with demanding callings, Sister Hinckley has spoken the right word to me or squeezed my trembling hand or—especially—written the encouraging, inspiring note which has given me hope, faith, courage, and confidence. I am sure if she has done this for me, she has done it for countless others.

Countless others will attest that Marjorie Hinckley has, indeed, encouraged and inspired them with her confidence and her understanding.

CHAPTER TEN

GRAND-MOTHERING

*

"I SOMETIMES THINK YOU ARE TOO GOOD TO BE TRUE"

The following excerpt from a letter to a granddaughter, Jennie H. Soulier, who was working in England at the time, introduces Marjorie Hinckley's attitude toward her role as a grandmother:

May 18, 1989

Your Mother's Day letter written on the 10th and mailed on the 12th arrived in today's mail. One week, which is quite wonderful service all the way from Coventry, England. This was a letter to warm my heart. This was a letter to make any rough roads we might have traveled to reach age seventy-seven worth it all. You gave me a Mother's Day supreme. A wonderful letter and a phone call. I ask myself what I ever could have done to deserve such a remarkable and beautiful and wonderful granddaughter! I sometimes think you are too good to be true. If only everyone in the world could have a granddaughter like you, what joy would be in the world. I don't know what to say except "I love you" and that seems so inadequate. Thank you for being what you are and for bringing so much joy into our lives.

Love,

Grandma.

Sister Hinckley's particular brand of grandmothering is one of camaraderie and support and encouragement. Maybe she learned this from her own mother, as suggested in this three-generation portrait drawn by daughter Jane H. Dudley:

It was a warm May afternoon. The school bell had rung for the close of the day, and the countdown for summer was on. My friend and I had big plans for after school. I would go home with her while she changed her clothes, and then she would go home with me. We could ride bikes until dinner. If we were lucky we could ride down to the root beer stand and buy a frosty mug. It all sounded too wonderful, so we picked up our pace.

As we turned into my friend's driveway, a sick feeling settled in the pit of our stomachs. We knew that our grand plans had been severely altered as we looked up and saw her grandma. She was the hardest-working woman I knew. She dripped with Comet cleanser and Slix furniture polish. This was a woman who greeted everyone with a rag. It didn't matter if you lived in the house or not, she assumed that you had come to clean. My friend and I knew that any plans we had made were over. I made up a feeble excuse that I had to go directly home and left. I didn't dare enter her house, knowing that I would become the next victim of the dust rag. "Call me when you can play," I said feebly.

I ran home ready to call someone else, wondering why my friend's grandma always broke the rules of grandmothering.

I bolted through the back door. "Hello," I yelled. "I'm home." There on the small sofa sat Grandma Pay. She was my mother's mother, and one of the sweetest and kindest persons I knew. Mother called from the kitchen, "Jane, make sure that you straighten your room before you go out to play." Grandma looked at me and said, "Oh, Marge, don't always be telling that child what to do. She has just had the longest day at school."

Now this, I thought, *is a true grandma!* A true grandma doesn't see any faults in you. Grandmas were placed on the earth to love and praise you. I knew then that I was one lucky person.

The years went by. My friend's grandma was still cleaning, and Grandma Pay was still sitting on the sofa telling me what a nice person I was. I loved that little woman. I hoped that one day my children would have a grandma who loved them unconditionally, not for what they accomplished.

Yesterday the back door flew open, and my daughter, Sarah, ran in from school. She came in the family room and there was Grandma Hinckley sitting on the sofa. "Hi, Grandma," Sarah said. "Well, hello, Sarah, you look so beautiful today. Did you have a nice day?" was the reply. I walked into the room and said, "Hello, Sarah, make sure you put your backpack away." I could say that. I was the mom and my mother was the grandma.

Sarah has a real grandma. She knows the rules and abides by them. "Lift up your head and be of good cheer" is her motto. My children love her. They will always carry with them wonderful memories of Grandma Hinckley. She has showered them with trinkets from foreign lands, thrown Christmas parties just for them, taken them on shopping sprees at ZCMI, and bought them candy bars at the grocery store. Most of all, she has praised and loved them. Grandma is their biggest fan, and they in turn are hers.

Grandma Hinckley not only loves her grandchildren, she loves everyone: missionaries, sons-in-law, daughters-in-law, neighbors, and the clerk in the store. She has grown old through the years and is sitting on the small sofa more and more. However, she will always have a kind word to say. She knows the rules and rights of grandmothering, and that is how it should be.

This "I'm on your team" spirit infuses all of Grandma Hinckley's interactions with her grandchildren. There's never a hint of "What's the matter with this younger generation?" Just expressions of confidence and a feeling of mutual enjoyment. As Jessica Dudley, a granddaughter, says:

Grandma Hinckley always makes you feel like you are the most important person in the world. When you are talking with her, nothing else matters. Some of my favorite memories with Grandma are when I have just dropped by their apartment to say hi. Grandma will stop whatever she's doing just to chat with me. We'll talk about everything and nothing. We'll laugh about anything. When you're in Grandma's presence, everything you have to say is important.

Amy Pearce, a granddaughter, remembers the comfort of her grandmother's love:

While on my mission in Germany I received a package from my brother for my birthday. It was a bag of pink mints, with a note: "I couldn't think of a better gift than a touch of home: Grandma and

Grandpa Hinckley. Let the flavored sugar carry you away into a world of comfort and love on East Capitol Blvd."

My brother was right. "A world of comfort and love." The candies are my childhood at Grandma and Grandpa's house in tasteable form. There has always been, ever since I can remember, a dish of thick pink mints—each one about the diameter of a nickel—on the table in their living room. And a spare bag or two in the chest of drawers next to the wall. Yes, we children discovered their hiding place many, many years ago.

I took my brother's advice, putting a few mints in my pocket as we tracted up and down the drizzly streets of Germany that winter. Every time I would pop one into my mouth, I was instantly back in the comfort of Grandma and Grandpa's love.

Elizabeth Hinckley, a granddaughter, remembers:

Once I made a mistake at Grandma's house. I felt really, really scared and I wanted to disappear, shrivel up, and hide in the corner. But Grandma and my aunt Jane laughed and said, "Lizzie, don't worry." They told me it was okay and didn't matter. No one held it against me or even remembered it five minutes later.

Joseph B. Hinckley describes his grandmother:

She's fun, she's cute, she's very talkative. She gets around town. Anyplace you go with her is fun. She likes to visit with her grandkids and know what we're doing, how we're doing in school, and anything else we're up to. She thinks we're great!

Another grandson, Spencer Hinckley, says:

The most outstanding characteristic of Grandma is that she is always happy and positive. She is always smiling, and you can't keep from smiling when you're around her. She is always just so happy to be there—no matter where she is. I suppose that is evidence of her quiet testimony of the gospel. It emanates from her countenance. I love her.

And granddaughter Ada Hinckley concurs:

She is always smiling, and when you think of her it makes you smile!

Celia B. Benson remembers her grandmother as a close friend:

There has never been a generation gap between Grandma Hinckley and her grandchildren. She isn't the typical grandmother who bakes homemade gingerbread cookies and sits in a rocker and knits. Growing up she was more of a best friend than a grand-mother. That explains why we called her our "groovy grandma."

I'll never forget how when I was ten years old Grandma took my cousin Rosemary and me to ZCMI to pick out matching outfits for our first day of fifth grade. I couldn't believe it because the shirt, sweater, and pants all matched—and they weren't even on sale! Being the third girl in the family, I was used to hand-me-downs, so this was a big deal for me. Grandma then took us to the ZCMI beauty parlor to get a manicure and then to lunch at the Tiffin Room. We felt like princesses for a day. We were sure that nothing we did the rest of our lives would compare with that one day. We had been treated like royalty and could now die happy.

Granddaughter Katie B. Wright says:

Grandma Hinckley is as thoughtful and generous as any person I have known. She has a way of making you think you are the greatest. She does it in little ways, like taking you to lunch or sending a note in the mail.

I remember sleeping over at Grandma's and the next day she took me to ZCMI. We had lunch in the basement and then she bought us an extra sweet at the bakery. (Grandma loves sweets.) I felt spoiled!

Angela B. Folsom found her grandmother to be a motivating teacher:

Grandma cultivated in me a love for the hymns of the Church. As I progressed in my piano playing so that I could play the hymns, she challenged me to memorize the words also. Every time I had memorized all the verses to a hymn, I was to sing it to her. She would then give me a reward.

Around age eight, I remember standing in her living room near her piano, singing "I Stand All Amazed" and "When upon Life's Billows." Those were also the first two hymns I had learned how to play, and I was so pleased. I don't remember what I received as a "reward," or even if I received anything, for knowing all the verses. What she taught me, however, was the importance of hymns and music in our lives. She often told me during those times together, "If you are going to be a member of this church, you need to learn the hymns. There will be many times in your life where hymnbooks won't be available (such as general conference) and you will want to be able to sing." I cherish the advice she gave me at such a young age.

Amy Pearce remembers her grandmother's warmth:

I remember sitting in church as a young child and looking at all of the older women in our ward. Some of them had such bony laps and arms or pointed noses and chins. Some were tall and had long hair. I couldn't help but make comparisons between these grandmas and my own Grandma Hinckley. I'm always convinced that my grandma came right out of the storybook encyclopedia that describes what the perfect grandma is like. She is round and soft in the places that grandmas should be. Her lap is comfortable to sit on; she has the perfect amount of wrinkles, gray hair, and glasses; and she is always smiling—even when she drifts asleep.

When I would sit on Grandma's lap, I always felt like the blue-ribbon winner at the state fair. Grandma would examine my hands and fingers, telling me that they were the most beautiful hands she had ever seen. What she wouldn't give to have fingers like mine! How incredibly lucky I was to have such wonderful nails! My eyelashes were always long and beautiful, my feet were perfect for the sand and water of the beach, and even my multitude of freckles were a blessing. She would run her fingers through my hair, praising its thickness and color. This went on and on. With each thing she would mention, I felt like I must have been the only one in the whole world to have dimples or strong legs or two of the best climbing arms or whatever it was that happened to be showcased at the moment. What blessings! What a special person I was! She would always say, "Best of all, you have a great personality."

Grandma is always praising. She can turn anyone from an ugly frog into an elegant prince. She is observant. She notices everything and she never hesitates to point out the positive points. These little positive points may be very obvious, but therein lies the charm. She is taken back and impressed with the obvious. Nothing and no one is too small or insignificant for her praise.

Grandson Hobie Hinckley says:

One thing I really love about Grandma is her humility and gratitude. She usually mentions in letters she writes, "Oh, I have such wonderful grandchildren. I just hope I can live worthy of them!" That is always a great boost, with such a wonderful person as Grandma saying she hopes to live worthy of us grandchildren! I always feel that it should be the other way around, because she is such a spiritual person, and a great example to all of us.

Heather B. Blair, a granddaughter, remembers some special teaching moments:

Marjorie Pay Hinckley is a women of culture and refinement, and she wanted her grandchildren to have a taste for culture also. One of my treasured memories is of taking elocution lessons from Grandma. When I was about ten years old, we began weekly elocution lessons. We started with the basics: "She sells sea shells by the sea shore," and "Eight great gray geese gazing gaily into Greece." I would stand in the front hall while Grandma sat at the far end of the living room, and I would recite these things to her until they were considered perfect. We would then read poetry together and choose one or two poems that I would memorize for next week's lesson. They would be poems like Robert Louis Stevenson's "The Swing" or "I Have a Little Shadow." She taught me diction, composure, how to look at an audience without really looking at them, and much more. She helped me learn proper pronunciation and diction, where and when to emphasize words, and how to organize and write a talk.

We would read literature together for her Relief Society lessons. I can still vividly see us sitting together at the round table in her kitchen reading Robert Frost's "Death of the Hired Man" and crying together at the end of it. To this day, we still enjoy reading it together. She taught me to love great literature and fine arts.

Emily P. Fox remembers the wonderful freedom of going to Grandma's house as a child:

There was such freedom at Grandma Hinckley's house. I don't ever remember her reminding us of the rules—rules, what a strange idea—or limiting our fun with warnings and nagging. As soon as we arrived, the cousins would run down the basement stairs, out onto the back patio where our parents and grandparents were visiting, then down the weeded hill that led to the canyon below. Making our way through the weeds, dirt, and rocks, we stopped partway down the steep hill where the terrain flattened out. We would spend unclocked hours there. It was our own little world where we created anything our minds could imagine. We sectioned off the "rooms" in our "houses" with large sticks or short ones put end to end. We built sinks, digging away dirt for the basin and outlining the hole with rocks. We made chairs from larger rocks or large green leaves if any could be found.

Soon, someone from the patio level would come down with an ice-cream cone in hand and we knew dessert was being served. There weren't even interrupting announcements about dessert being ready. We would just make our way up the hill whenever we could take a break, to grab a cone and then return to continue our serious work. Grandma's was a magical place where we felt a peaceful, happy freedom.

Amy Pearce, another granddaughter, remembers the inside of Grandma's house:

Grandma's house was full of treasures. They had collected a variety of exotic things over the years from their many travels. Little, shiny wooden boxes with inlaid mother-of-pearl and ancient calculators from Asia, colorful masks from South America, music boxes from Germany, carved figurines and porcelain elephants from Indonesia, paintings, baskets, and so on. She had two woven pieces from the Orient hanging on the wall in her entryway. They were each two or three feet long, with red and purple tassels hanging from them. A few of my girl cousins and I would play with the tassels for hours. I loved the way they would smoothly and quickly slip through my fingers. It was on these tassels that I learned how to braid.

I don't know if Grandma ever saw us playing with the tassels—or anything else, for that matter. She never said anything to us about it. When we left her house, the tassels would always be braided or twisted in the newly discovered way of the day, and always upon our return they would be hanging orderly and straight again. So I guess she knew about our work. When I think of this now, I can't believe that it didn't drive Grandma nuts—little dirty hands and fingers mauling the silky tassels and wooden figurines? But that was the magic in it. Grandma had trust and confidence in us. Her house wasn't just a museum for preserving and protecting interesting artifacts, it was a magical world where we were always welcome to learn and explore.

Ann Hinckley, a granddaughter, recalls:

After living far away from grandparents for most of my life, we finally moved back to Salt Lake City the summer before I started college. I just couldn't get enough of Grandma and spent many of those summer days at her house. We talked of my plans and her memories, thumbed through her high-school yearbooks, folded loads of laundry, looked at souvenirs from the far-off lands she had visited, went grocery shopping for miniature bottles of milk and half cartons of eggs, took naps, and made memories. It's always good to be with Grandma.

Celia B. Benson describes her grandmother's letters:

Grandma Hinckley was an avid letter writer. She filled our mailboxes with vivid details of her travels across the continents. Her detailed descriptions of people and places came alive to us as we experienced the sights and sounds of many faraway lands. When she wasn't traveling, she continued to fill our mailboxes with notes and cards carrying words of encouragement. Grandma was always our greatest cheerleader. She had a way of saying just the right thing at the right time to make you feel like you could conquer the world— or at least make it through the day. Through the years her notes and cards have become little pillars of strength to buoy me up in times of need, or just to remind me that somewhere there is someone who thinks I'm okay.

A few letters and postcards from Grandma Hinckley demonstrate this skill of long-distance grandmothering:

Nov. 27, 1980

Dear Celia,

Happy birthday! Please get something for you with this money. I realize it will not buy much more than a double-decker cone on today's market, but know that my love for you is also keeping up with inflation—it triples with each passing year.

XOXO,

G. Hinckley

*****

February 22, 1985

Dear Holly, Annie, Spencer, and Ada,

Your report cards were simply outstanding. You are all very smart, but even better than being smart is that you work hard, and that is the most impressive of all. Rosemary had a great report card like you and I said, "Oh, Rosie, you are so smart," and she replied, "I'm not so smart, I just work hard." That is even better than being smart. However, you are all very smart and you all work hard and that is a great combination. Even better than that is that you are all good children, and that is the most important of all. When I consider that we have 23 grandchildren and not one problem child I feel like the most blessed grandmother in the whole world. You are like 23 angels right out of heaven. I don't know what we have done to deserve you.

I will be returning your report cards with some other material in a few days. You will want to keep them.

We love you, love you, love you!

Grandma H.

P.S. A kiss for Joseph. XO

*****

February 22, 1981

Dear Holly,

While Grandpa was in a meeting Friday afternoon I walked through the Polynesian Center for two hours with some friends and decided this is a place where we should have a cousin's party. Maybe someday!

Love,

M.

*****

Pusan, Korea, May 31, 1980

Dear Emily,

There are hundreds of people on the beach today, but I have not seen one swim suit. The women are all in dresses, carrying their shoes in their hands and holding up their skirts while they wade out in the water. When the waves come up to their knees they scream and run back. It is hard to enjoy this alone. As I walked along the beach I pretended one of you was with me.

Love,

G. Hinckley

*****

Visits to grandchildren have been no less effective than letters. Even though a visit cannot be read and reread, the confidence Grandma Hinckley always instills seems to last a very long time. Jeff Barnes, a grandson, talks about one such visit:

I had been in the mission field just six weeks when Grandma and Grandpa came to Poland with the Tabernacle Choir. I was still in a state of bewilderment, still adjusting to the food, the surroundings, and the language in that strange and very foreign land.

Grandpa held a meeting with the missionaries. It was a new mission, and there were only about twenty-five of us at the time, including some couples and the mission president. The meeting was held in the Marriott Hotel in Warsaw. We all had lunch with Grandma and Grandpa, and then we had a short meeting.

The minute the closing prayer was said, Grandma made a beeline for me. "Get your companion," she said, "and follow me." She then led us upstairs to her room and began unloading her bag. She handed us toiletry kits and slippers from the airlines. She gave us two tubes of toothpaste and some little bottles of shampoo. She was also carrying a little package from my parents. It was all like manna from heaven because those items were still extremely scarce in Poland.

She then sat down and gave me the greatest gift of all—her time and her genuine interest and love. She wanted to know how I was *really* doing. Was I happy? Was I eating right? How was the language coming? Was I getting my rest? Did I need anything?

She left me with reassuring words. She believed in me and just knew I was going to be a great missionary!

When we parted that day, I was renewed. It meant so much to me to have had that brief interlude. I left knowing that I wanted to be a great missionary!

A journal entry from another grandson, Jonathan Dudley, describes his grandparents' visit to his mission.

August 30, 1995

Grandma and Grandpa were here today. They are so busy. Grandpa dedicated the new Hyde Park chapel. They both spoke and did a great job. Grandpa did fine but Grandma was the best. Everyone loved her, and all the missionaries commented to me how hilarious she was. On Monday afternoon we held a mission conference. Once again, Grandma was the star. I spoke to them for a minute after the meeting, and then they left for Cambridge. They keep a crazy schedule. I am so lucky to have them both. It was fun to see them.

Granddaughter Rosemary P. Olsen also treasured her grandparents' visits:

My husband and I were living in Sacramento, California, while he was completing his training. It was the first time in my life that I had lived away from my family and I missed them terribly. Not only was I used to being near my immediate family but there was also a lot of interaction with extended family, including my grandparents, that I missed. Visitors for me were like a little piece of heaven.

So you can imagine how excited I was when I heard that my grandparents would be at our Sacramento regional conference. Their schedule, as usual, was to be very full, but Grandpa called to say that he thought they could come to breakfast Sunday morning before the meeting. We were thrilled.

Then, on Saturday, they called to say that a media interview had been set up on Sunday morning. He wouldn't be able to come to my house, but could I find a way to pick Grandma up during the priesthood leadership session? Could I find a way? You bet!

167

She was darling, as usual. Fussed over me and my children. Loved my house. Visited and visited. It was wonderful.

Grandpa, amazingly, seems to make it to all of the blessings, baptisms, and weddings. I don't know how he does it. But if there is ever any slack to be taken up in the family, Grandma is ready and eager to do it. Maybe she is the reason that none of us has ever felt neglected or resentful. It is through Grandma's visits, letters, and telephone calls that we have experienced the wonder and majesty of my grandfather's great efforts in doing the Lord's work.

She is contagiously optimistic about everyone and everything. Through her telephone calls she fills me in on my cousins and aunts and uncles. She keeps me connected with them and their lives, sharing funny stories of my cousin's children, where an uncle is traveling, or about the nice boy my cousin is dating. She is the glue that keeps our family together.

Ann Hinckley, a granddaughter, reminisces:

Pink lemonade and lamb always remind me of Grandma. Growing up in Michigan, we spent very few holidays with faraway grandparents and cousins, but I do remember one Easter Sunday at Grandma's. Even though my siblings and I were all very young, she sat us at her large dining-room table—just like the adults—for Easter dinner. Her fine china and goblets sparkled. The tablecloth was pink, the napkins were pink, even the lemonade was pink. It was breathtakingly wonderful to me. Something about the novelty of drinking lemonade with dinner, or tasting lamb and mint jelly for the very first time—or it very well may have been the beauty of everything pink. But it was magic. I felt absolutely like royalty. I still never eat lamb without wishing for pink lemonade, and lemonade always tastes better with lamb. They are meant for each other. And they will always remind me of Grandma.

If the grandchildren had to pinpoint one time of year that reminds them of Grandma, it would have to be Christmas. This is her holiday. Everything she does with it is magical. Around the beginning of December, little cards arrive every four or five days in the mail. Each child remembers the excitement of getting a card with just his or her own name on it. If you lived out of town, it was added reassurance that Grandma always thought about you even if you didn't see her very often.

And these aren't ordinary cards. They pop out or stand up or play a Christmas carol. Lizzie even remembers one that her brother received that unfolded into a Santa mask. The cards usually contain one or two sentences at most, things like: "Good things happen at Christmastime" or "From your secret elf" or "Start counting the days" or just a simple "XOXO." She usually doesn't sign her name, but the small, cursive penmanship is very familiar.

Somewhere in between all of the cards is an invitation to the Grandchildren's Christmas Party: "Attendance mandatory" or "Only the chicken pox will qualify as an excuse." Christmas anticipation doesn't get any better than that.

Sunday, December 18, 5:30 P.M.
Christmas dinner and fish pond.
Walk through Temple Square.
Try, try, try to be there!
Love,
Grandma H.

Thursday, December 22, 7:00 P.M.
Walk through Temple Square if we didn't make it on the 18th.
Sleepover.

Breakfast.

"Annie" at Promised Valley Playhouse.

4:00 P.M. Straight home!

Love,

G. Hinckley

Michael Hinckley, a grandson, remembers these extraordinary parties:

My earliest and clearest memories of Grandma are the "Cousins' Christmas Parties," which were an essential part of each Christmas season. The magic of the Christmas season is already prevalent in the lives of children, yet this annual gala put on by Grandma added even more excitement. First of all, the simple fact that Grandma would invite only the grandchildren to come to the party was something significant in itself. While at family dinners we kids were always at the "children's tables," such was not the case on this occasion. There were no adults—only Grandma. We children all sat together at the "adults' table." We were the important people.

The tables were festively decorated with linens of green and red, plates portraying Christmas scenes and symbols, and other articles ornamenting each dining place. Perhaps the most exciting feature of the dinner table was the shiny Christmas-tree ornament decorating the place of each grandchild. (I still have all of these, and I will pass them on to my children.) Inevitably, these were the most beautiful ornaments we would place on our trees each year. Usually Grandma had purchased them earlier in the year in some foreign country.

Before we ate, Grandpa gave us a little manners lesson. Apparently our manners, or rather our lack of manners, were the reason Grandma began having the parties! I'm not sure our manners improved, but some of my cousins remember specific rules: no elbows on the table, don't reach across someone to get food, say "I'm finished, thank you," rather than "I'm all done!"

The dinner itself was an event to be remembered. Fruit cocktail in stemmed sherbet glasses, ham, potatoes, corn, rolls (with raspberry jam), and an array of other vegetables, meat, and delicious foods. The desserts would vary from ice cream to cakes, pies, cookies, and so on. Yes, the food was spectacular, but the real fun was after dinner.

We started with several games of Bingo. Grandma would call the numbers as we placed our pieces down on the appropriate squares, each child hoping he or she would be next to yell "Bingo!" There were prizes for those who won. And for those who didn't win, there were still prizes. Everyone's a winner with Grandma.

Next was the "fish pond." Grandpa had already wired an elaborate "fishing pole" together and strung a blanket across a door opening. Grandma sat on the other side of the blanket. Each child cast, waited for Grandma to secure the gift (each suited to the individual child), and then "reeled in." The fishing was always good!

As evening wore on and we had all prepared for bed, we would lie down in our sleeping bags behind doors, under the piano, on the sofa, or in any other creative spot we could find with a cousin or two. Then Grandma would read to us, the same wonderful Christmas stories every year. They made us feel warm inside. After she finished reading, she would sit absolutely still in a chair until every one of us was sound asleep. One time when she started to tiptoe through us to get back upstairs, my sister said, "I'm still awake!" So she sat down and read her favorite story, *The Little Match Girl*, all the way through again.

The next morning it was breakfast, and then sometimes she had tickets to a Christmas play for all of us. By the time our parents picked us up, we were finished with the best part of December.

The Christmas parties still go on now, but they're no longer sleepovers. Every grandchild, including spouses and great-grandchildren, comes to the festive dinner and enjoys Bingo and the fish pond. We love being together.

Of course, every year Grandpa says: "Now, you kids know that this is the last Christmas party. There are too many of you, you're too noisy, and it's just too much work for your grandma!"

We just laugh and wait eleven months for the invitations to come in the mail.

Ada Hinckley remembers that Grandma found a way of including even the out-of-town grandchildren in the Christmas parties:

I remember when we were little and lived away from Salt Lake City, we would anticipate the fish-pond box in the mail with our wrapped presents, and we would open them as a family the same night that all of our cousins did at Grandma's house. Although we lived away from our cousins and grandparents for a time, we never felt left out of the festivities, because we would always get to be a part of the fish pond. Many times we received a doll or an ornament from an exotic part of the world she and Grandpa had been to earlier in the year. We all have a great collection of ornaments from Grandma, and every year when we put them on the Christmas tree we remember the year we got each of them and the different countries they are from.

Granddaughter Elizabeth Hinckley has similar memories:

Even when we lived in Arizona, Grandma always thought of us and included us. At Christmastime, when all the cousins did fish pond, she would send us our fish-pond presents in the mail. She would send us Christmas cards throughout the whole Christmas season. We always loved to get her cards and presents.

Grandma Hinckley also collected many dolls herself, as Holly Hinckley, a granddaughter, remembers:

One of my favorite Grandma Hinckley memories is playing with her doll collection in the basement of the house on East Capitol Boulevard. We would take out each doll, and Grandma would tell us where the doll came from and the story of her trip to that country. She has dolls from everywhere: Fiji, Argentina, the Philippines, Norway, Hong Kong, Korea, Finland—places I had never even heard of at that age. She would tell us all about that country, the people there, her experiences with them, the native costumes, and so on. We would take our favorite dolls out over and over again to hear the stories. One day we pulled out a rather ordinary-looking doll and asked where it came from. "ZCMI," was the answer. We laughed hysterically. We asked her over and over again where it came from, just to hear her say again, "ZCMI." Giggling with Grandma over whatever struck us as funny was even more fun than playing with her dolls.

The memory of playing dolls with Grandma in her basement came back to me years later when I was serving a mission in France.

In anticipation of Grandma and Grandpa's trip to Paris, my stake president called me to find out what he could offer them as a remembrance of their time in France. He wanted to know their tastes and if they collected anything. The one thing that came immediately to my mind was that my grandmother loved dolls from foreign countries. And so they presented her with a traditional French doll to add to her collection.

Another granddaughter, Mary Dudley, describes her feelings:

My grandma is the kindest person in the world. She loves all of God's creations, from a bird singing in the tree to the soft hug from a grandchild. She somehow knows just what to say or do in any situation. On many occasions you'll feel a soft hand slide into yours. That's the best feeling that anyone could ever have. I love her very, very much. Come rain or shine, I will always feel that soft hand in mine.

That gentle love shines through in a simple note to a granddaughter:

Thank you for the brief but wonderful visit yesterday morning. You brought sunshine that lasted all day and reminded me of the overwhelming blessing of 25 beautiful, perfect grandchildren. They are all so good I have to ask myself, "Can this be true?!"
Love,
Grandma

In the words of grandson Spencer Hinckley—words that speak for all twenty-five grandchildren:

She's nice. She's funny. And we love her.

CHAPTER
ELEVEN

REACHING OUT

*

"WE'RE ALL IN THIS TOGETHER"

Marjorie with Korean Saints

We all have a responsibility—a responsibility to make a difference, to be an influence, to lift someone. We are all in this together to work out our salvation, to reach our potential, and to be our brother's keeper. To help each other.

*****

Some years ago I had a friend who decided at the age of fifty that she was going to learn to play the piano. She courageously started out with *Thompson's Book I.* Each morning she went to the church at seven o'clock, where she would practice on the piano and the organ. After about a year they asked her to play a special number for one of the Relief Society lessons. She said she didn't feel ready, to give her another three months. The three months passed, and she consented to play a special number that she had memorized. This was her first public appearance on the piano. She started out beautifully. It went well for about three measures; then she lost it. Everything went blank. Her music teacher, who was present, said, "Don't be ruffled, Merle. Just start over." She started over and made it all the way through without a single mistake.

We have never loved Merle like we loved her that morning. Perhaps it was because she faltered a little in the beginning and we were all pulling for her, saying to ourselves, "Come on, Merle, you can do it." If her performance had been flawless from the start, we might all have been defensive and said, "Oh well, Merle can learn to play the piano because her husband is the kind who will get his own breakfast while she practices and her children don't make demands on her" and so on and so on and so on. As it was, she faltered a little, and we loved her the more. That experience has given me great comfort. I figure that if I fall a little short of what is expected of me, perhaps my sisters in the gospel will be compassionate and love me for trying.

It was Lucy Mack Smith who said, "Let us all help one another, that we may sit down together in heaven."

Marjorie Hinckley really believes that we're all great people. We're here to help each other, and that's that. With a charming kind of innocence, her glasses seem to see only the good in others. Not surprisingly, everyone behaves a little better in her presence. One of her children was complaining about someone one day and she said, "That's strange. She's always been so nice to me." The daughter shot back, "Oh, Mother. That doesn't mean anything. Who wouldn't be nice to you!"

In fact, everyone in The World According to Marjorie Hinckley is good.

By genetic predisposition or overwhelming compassion, she simply is unable to see bad in people. "Let's be kind to one another," she says, "for most of us are fighting a hard battle."

Augusto A. and Myrna M. Lim, president and matron of the Manila Philippines Temple, recall meeting Sister Hinckley for the first time:

The first time we remember meeting Sister Hinckley was in early 1965. It was just a few months after our baptisms, and the Hinckleys had come to the Philippines for a district conference. At the time President Lim was acting as the district clerk, and so our family was seated on the front row in front of the stage where the Hinckleys were seated. We remember that our second little daughter, Mitzi, was a little restless and went up on the stage. Sister Hinckley quickly picked her up and held her on her lap and entertained her through much of the meeting. She was so sweet and kind to this little child. That simple gesture let us know that she was one of us.

Angela B. Folsom, a granddaughter, confirms her grandmother's loving concern for the people she meets in her travels:

I remember the little notebook Grandma always brought home from a mission tour. It was filled with the names and phone numbers of parents of missionaries. She would spend whatever time it took telephoning mothers to let them know their missionaries were healthy and happy. It was just one more way she reached out to make the human connection.

Sister Hinckley expresses gratitude for the support we give one another in our ward families:

What a wonderful thing is a ward. It is like an extended family. Robert Frost, in his poem "The Death of the Hired Man," says, "Home is the place where, when you have to go there, They have to take you in." We have done a great deal of traveling in our lives. The best part of travel, of course, is coming home.

The first thing I do when I get home is touch base with my children. The next thing is to attend church in my very own ward, my very own Relief Society, and then I know that I am really home. It makes no difference whether it is a ward where we have lived for years or one we have recently moved into. I can remember a particular time when our ward had been recently divided. Because of other assignments, several weeks went by before I attended. When I returned to church it seemed that I knew only a handful of people. The rest were strangers. But do you know what? I still was thrilled to be back, because it was where I belonged, and that gave me a feeling of being home.

What a tremendous support system we have in one another. I have a friend named Sally. When I first met Sally she lived on the Isle of Wight, off the south coast of England. She was a member of a Protestant church. She lived in a large house on an estate with her husband, who was several years older than she, and her three young sons. One day she told me she had a terrible fear, a fear that her husband would die before her, and that her sons would grow up and leave the island, leaving her to grow old alone—no one to look after her or care about her.

"Doesn't that worry you?" she asked.

"No," I replied, "because if all my children moved away I would still have a bishop who would care about me and home teachers who would care about me and Relief Society visiting teachers who would really care about me."

It began to happen just as she feared. The sons came to America to be educated, eventually marrying and settling here. Her husband died. But the happy ending is that the sons, one by one, heard the gospel and joined the Church. Sally came to America. Her children taught her the gospel and she joined the Church. Her second son is now her bishop. She is a member of a ward in The Church of Jesus Christ of Latter-day Saints. She is no longer afraid.

Sister Hinckley describes how our sisterhood and brotherhood in the gospel bridges the superficial differences between people:

When Brother Hinckley had the responsibility for the work in Asia, our children were young and I didn't travel with him often. As they grew older, I began to go more often. But I will never forget my first trip to Hong Kong.

We arrived at the mission home in the early evening and had just put our bags down in the room assigned to us when the mission president's wife knocked on the door. She said, "Sister Hinckley, there is something I think I should tell you. There is a reception tonight in the mission home for many of the members. A very important lady will be here. She is Chinese, educated in Burma, a very prominent woman in community affairs, playing an important role in the United Nations Committee of Hong Kong. She has been ill and has not been out of the house for six months. Her doctor has given her permission either to attend a United Nations banquet at the hotel tonight or to attend her church reception at the mission home. She has chosen to come here because, having seen an apostle, she wants to see what an apostle's wife looks like."

Terror struck my heart. Remember that I was relatively young and new at this. We had been traveling for ten days. There had been no time to shampoo my hair for ten days. My clothes were wrinkled. I had inadvertently left my dress shoes in the hotel in Okinawa. I had only my sturdy walking shoes. I looked in the mirror, and the only thing I could think of was that Cinderella had a fairy godmother. Where was mine?!

I did the best I could with what I had to work with and went out to meet this impressive woman. Fortunately, she could speak English, and I soon discovered that though there could not have been two women with more diverse backgrounds, we had everything in common. We both knew that Joseph Smith had a vision. She was my Relief Society sister. And she longed for her children to grow up in the faith.

What did I learn from this? That the gospel of Jesus Christ is the greatest common denominator on the face of the earth, and that when every knee shall bend and every tongue confess that Jesus is the Christ, there will be no divisions among us.

Even pictures of Sister Hinckley in the newspaper reach across the boundaries of age and distance, including individual people in one great church family.

Dear Sister Hinckley,

My name is Elizabeth Bouchelle. I am 13 years old and I live in Virginia. I just want you to know that I love you. You always seem to be smiling and enjoying all of the activities you go to with President Hinckley. I am always delighted to see pictures of you in the *Church*

News. I just wanted you to know how much I admire and appreciate all you do. Please remember that there is a little 13-year-old girl in Virginia who is praying for you.

Love,

Elizabeth Bouchelle

One final story, told by Marie Hafen, wife of Elder Bruce Hafen of the Seventy, shows how even in a huge, impersonal meeting hall, Sister Hinckley finds a way to make that small but vital connection, giving everyone the reassurance that we are all one great family. This incident took place at the conclusion of a member meeting in Australia, where more than six thousand Saints had gathered to hear from the prophet.

The meeting was over. The Saints were singing farewell as the Hinckleys stood smiling at the platform edge. Sister Hinckley took a step forward and motioned with her finger for ten-year-old James to come toward her. He looked around to see whom she was motioning to. As he realized he was the one, he pointed at himself with an incredulous "Who, me?" gesture. She nodded and smiled more broadly as her finger continued to motion him forward. Suddenly his face had the startled look of a kangaroo in the headlights.

A combination of ushers and family members hoisted James up onto the four-foot-high

platform. Sister Hinckley put her hands on his shoulders and said something like, "Young man, I've been watching you all through the fireside. You are wonderful. You paid perfect attention. How the Lord must love you. You are the future of the Church in this beautiful land of Australia. I just love you." And she hugged him.

When President Hinckley saw what was happening, he walked over to James and embraced him gently just as he left Marjorie's arms. James was still searching for something—anything—to say when the ushers carefully lifted him back to the playing floor to his family. I'll always remember that shining little moment, the picture of instant connection and intimate communication of genuine love. That image—the prophet's arms around a young LDS boy, made possible by Sister Hinckley's unaffected and spontaneous warmth—captures for me the spiritual heart of what the Hinckleys' visit meant to the Church members throughout Australia and New Zealand.

As the story was told to me by James's mother later, it seems that James had prayed prior to the meeting with great hope that he would have a chance to shake the prophet's hand. His mother had counseled him that this probably wouldn't be possible because of the thousands of people who would be in the hall. Sister Hinckley's beckoning gesture was an answer to a boy's prayer.

President Hinckley repeats over and over that we are one great family, ten million strong. Sister Hinckley's inspired gesture of inclusion and love was the practical application of her husband's teachings. We are all in this together: a prophet, his wife, you and I, and a little boy in Brisbane.

CHAPTER TWELVE

SYNERGY

*

MARJORIE PAY AND
GORDON B. HINCKLEY

183

*Support is a solid noun and a very active verb in all
of Marjorie Hinckley's relationships. However, it is
never more obvious than in her relationship with her
husband. On introducing Sister Hinckley to a large audience at
BYU, Patricia T. Holland described the support Sister Hinckley gives:*

In order to fortify the foundation of any lasting structure, a good
architect knows that by joining together two 2 x 4s of equal
strength, he can create a synergy so powerful that it doesn't just
double the strength, it quadruples it.

This is what the Lord has done with Marjorie Pay and Gordon
B. Hinckley. The synergy that exists between the two of them has
more than quadrupled in strength for the Church, for their home,
and for each other.

That support has been evident from the beginning years of President and Sister Hinckley's marriage. When in the summer of 1945 her husband was trying to decide whether to continue working for the Denver and Rio Grande Railroad or return to employment with the Church, Marjorie's response to the conflicting offers was a characteristic statement of practical and accommodating support:

As for the job, you had just better make up your mind to do the one which you enjoy the most, as you will spend quite a bit of your life working at it. As for me, I can make myself reasonably happy wherever you are, and as for the children, it is a question either way and is something we cannot possibly foretell, no matter how we speculate and wonder and worry.

Let's hurry and take up life together again. I like it better that way.

Sister Hinckley speaks of mutual respect in marriage:

I have been thinking back—way back to 1937. We were married during the Depression—"the bottom of the Depression," as my husband always says. Money was scarce, but we were full of hope and optimism. Those early days were not all blissful, but they were filled with determination and a great desire to establish a happy home. We loved each other, there was no doubt about that. But we also had to get used to each other. I think every couple has to get used to each other.

Early on I realized it would be better if we worked harder at getting accustomed to one another than constantly trying to change each other—which I discovered was impossible. Try not to be too demanding of one another. There must be a little give and take, and a great deal of flexibility, to make a happy home.

While it is important to be accommodating and flexible, of course we can draw the line when it is personally important for us to do so.

A son reflects on his mother's ability to draw that line:

Mother's independence is an interesting thing. She has always been supportive of Dad, but she is also the only person who can make him back down. If she told him, "You are not going to tear up the kitchen this week, and that is final," he didn't touch the kitchen. And it's not just that he gives in. He stops blustering and starts to chuckle, then turns and walks out of the room with admiration written all over his face! I think he loves the feisty, independent part of her.

Donna Packer, wife of President Boyd K. Packer of the Twelve, shares her admiration of Sister Hinckley's support of her husband and his calling:

My husband was sustained to be an Assistant to the Quorum of the Twelve and Gordon B. Hinckley was sustained as an Apostle on September 30, 1961. I felt this was an overwhelming responsibility to associate with the Brethren and their wives. I was eager to hear and remember every word and action of these more experienced sisters.

Sister Hinckley was one I watched and listened to. She had a delightful, natural sense of humor that made her approachable. As I nurtured that acquaintance, I found a depth that came from pioneer heritage and years of family and Church service.

One of her grandfathers, in the prime of life, was killed in the construction of the Manti Temple. Now alone, her grandmother became an exceptional example of a mother who had to adjust to experiences in life.

One day Sister David O. McKay, another wife whom we all greatly respected, gave a thought on the role of women that has stayed with me for nearly forty years. One of the things I remember her saying was, "It is the artful duty of a woman to adjust."

Sister Hinckley has been an outstanding model, one who adjusts her schedule and the family's schedule to meet the needs of her priesthood holder. Sister Hinckley's Church service has included total support for her very active husband.

Ruth Faust, wife of President James E. Faust, remembers:

During the time President Kimball and President Romney were ill and President Hinckley was carrying such a difficult burden in the First Presidency, Sister Hinckley asked if she could have a ride to a particular function with me. She said, "I'm not going to drive anymore." When I asked her why, she said that she had returned home a little late recently and her husband had told her how relieved he was and how much he worried when she was out in the car. "Well," she said, "I don't want to add to your problems. You can cross that worry right off your list. I'll quit driving."

I've thought many times about that unselfish gift, so quickly and easily given, and wondered if I could give up my independence that generously. Marjorie Hinckley is truly an elect lady.

Margaret D. Nadauld, wife of Elder Stephen C. Nadauld of the Seventy, recalls another occasion where Sister Hinckley put her personal life on hold for the sake of the work:

I will always treasure my memory of November in Nashville in

At LDSSA fireside, January 21, 1996

1991, and Marjorie Hinckley's eightieth birthday. It was a memorable occasion for us, as we were there on assignment with President and Sister Hinckley for the regional conference that weekend.

For the Sabbath, the Grand Old Opry auditorium had been transformed into a lovely meeting hall where Saints gathered by the hundreds. Flowers banked a large pulpit; hymns of Zion were sung; reverence abounded; and prayers were offered to the Lord in gratitude for His blessings on the Saints in that area.

There was a hush over the congregation as the prelude music ended and the conducting officer began this much-anticipated conference. During the preliminary portion of the meeting, time was turned over to a local stake president. He came to the pulpit, his arms filled with an elegant bouquet of beautiful, long-stemmed red roses. He asked Sister Hinckley to join him at the pulpit and presented that beautiful bouquet to her, wishing her a happy birthday from all assembled. He then proceeded to read a tribute that had been sent, along with the roses, by her children to be read in commemoration of her eightieth birthday.

It was a tender moment for all of us as we recognized that this was one of many, many instances when President and Sister Hinckley had been separated from their family on special occasions. The Hinckley children, however, were practiced at making ties strong even in absences. They had found a way to let their mother know of their devotion to her, their admiration for her, and their love for her, even though she was a thousand miles from home. They knew she would be in the presence of loving brothers and sisters who would indulge their sentimental moment.

Sister Hinckley received the gift of love with graciousness and responded with a comment typical of her: "Oh, to be sixty again!" Then this diminutive, exemplary, lovely woman spoke of the great joys of being married to a servant of our Heavenly Father and the experiences she had enjoyed traveling the world with him. Her eyes smiled in a permanent happy twinkle as she spoke. And we knew that, at least for the years since her husband had been called to the ministry, Sister Hinckley's personal interests had been put on hold for the sake of the things that were most important in her life, and that was just fine by her!

Sister Hinckley has pondered, probably more than once, on the role of the supporting wife.

In the book of Alma is a story that has fascinated me since I first read it. It is about a very colorful character named Moroni— not to be confused with the last survivor of the Nephites, who was also named Moroni. This man was a brilliant military commander, and he rose to be supreme commander of all the Nephite forces at the age of twenty-five. For the next fourteen years he was off to the wars continuously except for two very short periods of peace during which he worked feverishly at reinforcing the Nephite defenses. When peace finally came, he was thirty-nine years old, and the story goes that at the age of forty-three he died. Sometime before this he had given the chief command of the armies of the Nephites to his son Moronihah. Now, if he had a son, he had a wife. I've often wondered where she was and how she fared during those fourteen years of almost continuous warfare, and how she felt to have him die so soon after coming home. I am sure there are many, many stories of patience and sacrifice that have never been told. We each do our part, and we each have our story.

Sister Hinckley gives more than verbal encouragement and constant adjustments of energy and schedules to support her husband's demanding calling. She offers her natural gifts, not in competition but in partnership with her husband's. Theirs is a cooperative and complementary work effort, fit into a perfect rhythm by years of practice.

For instance, President Hinckley's efficient, time-oriented pace pushes him in and out of meetings with dispatch, but she good-humoredly goes more slowly, taking time to pay attention to those who are anxious to greet them. His natural reticence about giving or receiving lavish praise is compensated by her generous compliments about everything and everyone. His blustering remonstrances are offset by her good-natured soothings, "Now, just settle down."

Janet Lee, wife of the late Rex E. Lee, former president of Brigham Young University, describes these complementary roles:

The dedication of buildings is a major event at BYU. On one such occasion, Rex and I were waiting in a quiet room of the new building with President and Sister Hinckley. The dedication program was to begin in a few minutes, and President Hinckley was standing by a window watching students hurry to class. He spoke as though to no one, saying something about the young people looking different from the way they used to. I think he might have used the word *unkempt.* Sister Hinckley didn't miss a beat. In an instant she was at his side, and with a smile and a soft voice transformed the moment from bewilderment to bemused acceptance. "They are just fine," she told him. "That is simply the way young people like to dress today; they want to be comfortable. Think about how good they are."

There was not a hint of reproach in her voice. She had a way of defending the students with love and understanding, yet showing the same respect for anyone who viewed things differently. Those students had a friend in an eighty-two-year-old woman whose love for everyone united a prophet and his young followers that day.

And so there is a constant balance between the two of them—sometimes needing a little fine-tuning, but certainly creating a marvelous synergy.

As for Sister Hinckley's constant support of her husband—is she, as some in the world might suppose, erasing her own existence? Far from it! Although she is unselfish and other-centered, there doesn't seem to be a question of her own basic worth. Perhaps her sense of self is so fundamentally sound that she can be completely unselfish without losing even a particle of her real self.

Even though her husband's busy and demanding life requires a great deal of her time and energy, it has always been understood, by both of them, that she is an important individual:

Gordon always let me do my own thing. He never insisted that I do anything his way, or any way, for that matter. From the very beginning he gave me space and let me fly.

Another memory from Janet Lee illustrates the Hinckleys' mutually supportive relationship:

Once a year during my husband's administration, we had the honor of inviting General Authorities into our home for dinner. On one particular evening, the seating arrangements placed President and Sister Hinckley opposite each other instead of side by side at their table. I was unaware at the time, but it was a special day for the Hinckleys. In a few days I would learn that it had been their wedding anniversary.

In a devotional at BYU the next week, President Hinckley shared some reflections from that evening as he thought about his life with

Sister Hinckley. Listening to his words, I was tutored by the genuine tenderness of his message. I felt good about life in general: about what had been, what is now, and what will be. Hope and an understanding of the beauty of true and everlasting love replaced my fear of growing older. In his own words, President Hinckley described his wife in a way no one else could. Once again I was taught by her life to be content with what I am, always looking forward to being that better person I can become as the years go by.

President Hinckley began: "May I be personal for a moment? I sat at dinner across the table from my wife the other evening. It was fifty-five years ago that we were married in the Salt Lake Temple. The wondrous aura of young womanhood was upon her. She was beautiful, and I was bewitched. Now, for more than half a century, we have walked together through much of storm as well as sunshine. Today neither of us stands as tall as we once did. As I looked at her across the table, I noted a few wrinkles in her face and hands. But are they less beautiful than before? No, in fact, they are more so. Those wrinkles have a beauty of their own, and inherent in their very presence is something that speaks reassuringly of strength and integrity and a love that runs more deeply and quietly than ever before."

Always, I will remember the gentleness in his voice as he spoke. I have not been given the privilege of growing old with my eternal companion, but in my imagination I want to believe that if we had been able to celebrate fifty-five years of marriage, I could have deserved such a tribute.

All of the characteristics and gifts of Marjorie Pay Hinckley enrich and complement those of her husband, Gordon B. Hinckley. They bless his personal life as well as make it possible for him to do the things that the Lord has required of him.

Her faith stands as a supporting pillar next to his.

Her genuineness helps to nullify the poison of adulation, against which those in public life always have to be on guard.

Her remarkable aptitude for mothering has given him the reassurance that even in his absence his children have been taught, loved, and well cared for.

Her unfailing optimism and good cheer have buoyed him up and given him happy companionship during rigorous travel assignments.

Her constant expressions of gratitude and humility have brought a spirit of contentment into their relationship.

Her enthusiasm for new information, people, and places has been a match for her husband's.

Her ready humor has lightened his load and restored perspective.

Her listening and understanding ear have given him respite.

Her generous expressions of confidence and belief in his abilities have moved him forward.

Her attention to grandchildren has bound their hearts to him and to the gospel.

And, reaching beyond their immediate family, she has gone about the Church at his side, knitting our hearts together in unity and love—into one great family ten million strong.

EPILOGUE

TO MARJORIE

*

BY PRESIDENT GORDON B. HINCKLEY

My darling,

All that is said in this book concerning your virtues is true. Your own words and those spoken by a host of friends bear tribute to your worth. More, much more, might have been included.

It is now more than sixty years since we entered the Salt Lake Temple, there to be married for eternity. I had known you for a long time prior to that. I knew what I was getting into, and it has all turned out as I had hoped it would.

What a treasured companion you have been. Through all of these years we have walked side by side as equals before the Lord. There have been good days and bad days, but the good days have far outnumbered the bad ones.

Life for the most part has dealt gently with us. During the Depression, when we were newly married, we were poor and didn't know it because we were so rich in the things that really count. The laughter of happy children graced our kitchen table. The presence of a loving mother blessed our home. The Lord has opened the windows of heaven and showered down blessings too numerous to mention. He has smiled upon us in a wondrous way.

We have found comfort and gladness in one another and in our children. Now they have families of their own and grandchildren. All of our posterity have brought joy to our hearts.

When our children were young, you seldom traveled with me. I would be gone for as long as two months at a time. There were not even telephone calls permitted in those days. We wrote letters. You never complained. How wonderful it was to come home and be held warmly in your arms and those of our children.

Now in more recent years we have traveled far and wide together. We have visited every continent. We have held meetings in the great cities of the world and in many smaller ones. We have met the distinguished of the earth. We have spoken to millions who have appreciated you so greatly. With your familiar words you have won the love of all who have heard you. Your down-to-earth good sense, your sparkling and refreshing wit, your quiet and unfailing wisdom, and your tremendous and ever constant faith have won the hearts of all who have listened to you.

You have been my critic and my judge. You have seen to it that my shoes were shined, my suit pressed, my tie straight. You have pushed aside the flattery that comes with public life, and winnowed the kind and sincere words of honest and loving friends. You have held at bay that old fraud of adulation and kept my feet planted on the solid earth. How I appreciate you.

Your voracious appetite for reading and your relentless pursuit of knowledge have kept you alert and refreshing throughout a long and fruitful life.

Now we have grown old together, and it has been a sweet experience. We have shrunk in stature and move a little more slowly. We are more forgetful. But as of this writing we still have one another—and that is so good. And when in some future day the hand of death gently touches one or the other of us there will be tears, yes, but there will also be a quiet and certain assurance of reunion and eternal companionship.

"Trusty, dusky, vivid, true . . ."*

The God of Heaven fashioned you.

I love you, dear,

195

---

*From Robert Louis Stevenson, "To My Wife"

APPENDIX

*

TALKS GIVEN BY MARJORIE PAY HINCKLEY

WOMEN OF FAITH

ONE BEAUTIFUL spring Sunday morning in Brisbane, Australia, we were attending a stake conference. Although I had been invited to sit on the stand with my husband, I was relaxed, confident that I would not have to participate, as there was much stake business to be conducted. Suddenly I heard my name announced as the next speaker. I looked out at the audience of over a thousand people, my mind a complete blank. In the few seconds it took to walk the three or four steps to the pulpit, I remembered that my husband had said on a previous occasion, "If you have nothing to say, just bear your testimony." That was it. I would bear my testimony. So I expressed my love for the gospel and my gratitude for membership in the Church.

At the conclusion of the meeting a young woman of perhaps eighteen years of age said to me, "Sister Hinckley, you don't really appreciate the Church. You couldn't appreciate it the way I do, because you have always had it. I am a recent convert."

I was so taken back by the accusation that I could not think of an appropriate response. Only after we had parted company did I think of the things I could have said. I could have said, "My dear young friend, how could I not appreciate the gospel when I have seven ancestors who left their comfortable homes in

England at different times and came across the plains, some of them giving their lives for the cause?"

I could have told her that when I was a child, my father took me, together with my brother and sisters, to a spot in Emigration Canyon known as Little Mountain. There we sat on the rocks while Father told us that this was the approximate place where the handcart pioneers came down the canyon and into the valley in December of 1856. My grandmother was with them. They called her Polly. She was twelve years of age. On the trip across they had buried her sister Fanny, her brother James, and her six-week-old baby sister Edith, who was born during the journey.

Just hours before reaching the Salt Lake Valley, Polly's mother died. This young girl rode into the valley in one of the wagons, her feet frozen and her mother's earthly remains held tenderly across her lap. They arrived at nine o'clock at night, December 11, 1856. The next morning when Brigham Young came and saw their condition, three of the four survivors damaged by frost and their mother dead in the wagon, he wept. I quote from my grandmother's writings: "The doctor amputated my toes, while the sisters were dressing mother for her grave. When my feet were fixed they carried us in to see our mother for the last time. . . . Oh, how did we stand it. That afternoon mother was buried. I have thought often of my mother's words, 'Polly, I want to go to Zion while my children are small so that my children can be raised in the Gospel of Jesus Christ, for I know this is the true church.'"

I could have said to my sweet little convert friend, "Do you know what a profound effect this story of my grandmother had on my impressionable young mind, what feelings of pride and commitment and gratitude swelled in my heart?" With those early feelings of commitment, I determined to find a way to prove my faith.

Then I grew to adulthood. I had a wonderful marriage, children of my own, a comfortable life blessed with all the necessities and even some of the luxuries. I began to wonder how I could demonstrate my faith in such a convincing way as my grandmother and great-grandmother. As time went on this became more and more of a concern. Life was almost too good. I was even having feelings of guilt.

Then something wonderful happened. I learned about Charlotte. Charlotte Hyder Evans was my great-grandmother on my maternal line. Charlotte came across the plains also, when she was sixteen years old. The weather was favorable and they arrived safely, without undue hardship. Charlotte married a wonderful man and had twelve children. Like all other pioneer women, she went through the hardships incident to the building up of a new commonwealth—insufficient food, along with all kinds of sacrifices. She had her share of sorrow, sadness, and disappointment. She took care of the children and earned the living while her husband returned to England on a mission. At age forty-three she was widowed. She carried on with faith and with good cheer. When the Manti Temple was being built, she raised funds. When thread was needed, she tore up her skirt and gave the women wide strips to use as thread for sewing and mending. She made her adobe home a veritable palace with her beautiful handwork and flowers from her garden. When there were dead to be buried, she made burial clothes. When the call came for raising silkworms for the manufacture of silk, Charlotte was one of the first to plant two dozen mulberry trees to provide food for the silkworms. When the Relief Society was first organized, she became a visiting teacher, and she remained so for the rest of her life. Now, here was a woman I could relate to. Perhaps her contribution was not too dramatic or spectacular, but Charlotte did whatever needed to be done when it needed to be done. And, more importantly, she always did it with a cheerful heart. What more can any of us do?

Women of faith—they come in all ages and sizes. Even a child can show us the way.

Amy Eliza is nine. She is the sixth generation from Charlotte. She walked to the bishop's house with her parents one Sunday to pay her little tithing. On the way home, she asked, "What does the bishop do with our tithing money?" Her parents explained the many things that tithing is used for, including the building of temples. Four days later the building of a temple in Taiwan was announced. Amy Eliza was ecstatic. "Oh, thank goodness," she exclaimed. "They got my money just in time." Charlotte planted her mulberry trees. Amy Eliza made her contribution to the temple.

President Kimball said, "We are not asking for something spectacular, but rather for the women of the Church to find real self-fulfillment in the pursuit of righteousness in worthy endeavors."

A quote from Brigham Young, "Daily toil, however humble, is our daily duty and by doing it well we make it part of our daily worship."

And, I might add, part of our faith.

It is for us, brothers and sisters, to plant our own mulberry trees, making certain that underlying everything we do in the course of a day is a settled faith in God, in His existence, personality, and attributes. There must be faith in the restored gospel and in its power to save; faith in the divine mission of the Savior. This faith will give us the power to work righteousness.

God bless us all to do what needs to be done by our hands, and to do it cheerfully and with joy.

I HAVE HEARD ANGELS SING

WHEN I WAS A YOUNG GIRL of about twelve years of age, our Sunday School teacher told us in class one morning that the angels of heaven sang at the dedication of the Manti Temple. I could scarcely believe this.

Grandmother Paxman was living with us at the time, and I knew that she had been to the dedication of that temple. So I hurried home to ask her about it. I said rather apprehensively, "Grandmother, did you hear angels sing at the dedication of the Manti Temple?" She said, "I certainly did." And then she proceeded to tell me that before the service began, while the people were still assembling, she heard beautiful choir music. It sounded as if it were coming from an upstairs room, and she thought the choir was rehearsing. She said, "I wondered why a choir that could sing so beautifully would have to rehearse." Then, she said, "I noticed that the choir members were just taking their seats and were not singing at all, and I knew I had heard angels."

I was so impressed with this story. And I hoped that I might live so that someday I might see such a miracle. Many, many years—even decades—have passed and I have not heard angels sing like my grandmother did, nor have I witnessed any other spectacular miracle. And I am grateful. My testimony has been fed by small, simple, and sometimes seemingly unimportant experiences. I think this is as it should be. There are very few big and spectacular miracles in most of our lives. But it is a quiet multitude of little miracles that makes life sweet and adds to our testimonies. It is walking up a narrow, steep, back road on the island of Okinawa at seven o'clock in the morning and hearing the strains of a Mormon hymn come out of a squeaky pump organ. It is seeing the beautiful countenance of a Chinese man who sells fish on the streets of Aberdeen, as he stands to conduct a little sacrament meeting, in all the dignity of his calling. It is seeing the determination on the face of a young elder when he faces the difficulty of learning a new language and says, with fear and trembling but with great determination, "I'm going to lick this if it kills me." It's seeing a young father and mother drive fourteen hundred miles through the expanses of Australia with four boys under six years of age to attend a stake conference, and finding that the mother can still smile.

I wish to share with you a few angel voices I have figuratively heard sing. The experiences were sometimes small, but each one has helped me to believe.

Brother Hinckley has had the responsibility of the missions of the Orient for the past two years. Last year, I had the privilege of going with him through these missions in the early spring and again in November. Then, two months ago, on the fourteenth of April, we visited stake conferences and met with the missionaries in many of the islands of the South Pacific and in New Zealand and Australia and then went up to Bangkok, Singapore, and Saigon, Vietnam, to meet with the members of the Church who are in that area serving in the armed forces of the United States.

Our first stop was in Samoa, where there is a wonderful stake of Zion, presided over by a distinguished-looking gentleman who is part Samoan and part Chinese. We were not able to be there on a Sunday, so the first session of conference was held on Monday night. It was very hot and steamy. We were tired, not having seen a bed since Saturday night. We had to speak through translators, and it was a difficult experience, but the people were patient and they came back to the second session on Tuesday night. We expected to have four days in Samoa, but our flight out was canceled and we had to content ourselves to stay for a full week. This was very difficult for my husband because he had a tight schedule for the next five weeks, which all went under the bridge. But it wasn't really too painful for me.

Life in Samoa is very colorful. Most live in open-air *falles*. This affords no privacy for the family, but makes for very interesting sight-seeing on the part of the visitor. It was wonderfully interesting to roam around watching the people shred coconut and dry cocoa beans. Also, this gave us additional time to meet with the missionaries laboring in Samoa. There were about a hundred missionaries in this mission, thirty-five of them from the United States and the others local Samoans serving full-time. The Church also maintained three schools in Samoa, and because of the delay we had the pleasure of visiting the students in all three schools.

We went over to the island of Savaii and drove up into the hills, covered with coconut plantations and other beautiful tropical foliage, to visit the school at Viola. They were not expecting us, but thirty minutes after we arrived, they had the entire student body assembled in the auditorium, which was a roof with open sides. When we arrived at the auditorium, there were two hundred students, from the first grade through sixth, sitting on the floor with crossed legs in poker-straight lines. It was a sight to behold. They sang two songs—something about "love under the apple tree" and a religious number. Then a few speeches from the visitors. Then they marched by, each shaking hands with us as they sang a beautiful Samoan song, "Goodbye, my *felenie*," or "Good-bye, my friend, I never will forget you." They sounded like angels to me.

The next morning at the village, down on the lagoon, there was a district conference scheduled. We went to bed early, hoping for a good night's rest before all of the scheduled meetings. At three A.M. the whole village seemed to come alive. People were chattering like magpies. We could hear water splashing. I got up and looked out the window at the back of our room and discovered that the water of the lagoon was about twelve feet from my bed. There were at least a dozen Samoan boys swimming and laughing and playing in the water like it was noonday. Trucks came and went, and we learned later that Saints were beginning to arrive for the next day's meeting. We tried to ignore it and pretend that it was still night. At four A.M., everything still pitch dark, a choir of perhaps thirty young voices began to practice "High on the Mountain Top." Over and over and over again they sang it. "Surely this isn't actually happening," I said. Choirs don't practice at four A.M., even on the island of Savaii, Samoa. By five o'clock we couldn't fight it any longer, so we got dressed and went out to join in. By this time there were another twenty or so youngsters jumping up and down in a deep pool of water just beyond our front door, brushing their teeth, shampooing their hair, pushing each other in, scrubbing their elbows with coconut fiber. By ten o'clock that Saturday morning all were clean and shining and sitting quietly in the chapel for the first

207

session of their district conference. It was a sweet experience to see the influence of the Church of Jesus Christ on that isolated island of the Pacific where life is so different.

The next stake conference was held in New Zealand. As we sat on the stand and looked over that large congregation of over 1,000—some Caucasian and some Maori—a flood of memories swept over me of the first time I had been in New Zealand, five years before. It was for the dedication of the temple. My mind went back to those days.

I thought of the little woman from the South Island who sat in the temple chapel prior to going through for her endowments. In her hand she clutched a straw bag from which was bulging her Book of Remembrance. One could only guess at the years of preparation that had gone into that book, culminating in her trip to the temple.

I thought of the Maori lady who had given birth to seventeen children and who knelt at the altar of the temple during the first days of its opening to be sealed to those children and to her husband who had been many years gone.

I saw again Millie Tanio, who during those hectic days of open houses and dedication had kept the temple clean and sparkling as a diamond. Millie was half Maori, and until construction of the temple began, she lived in a fishing village with her husband, Joe, who walked with a limp from a high-school rugby injury. When the temple was being built, they left their home and came to Hamilton to work on the construction. When it was complete, they stayed on to act as custodians. How proud they were of this assignment. "If I never get to heaven, it doesn't matter," Millie said. "I'm having my heaven right here." Does she sound like an angel to you? She did to me.

I thought of other lessons I had learned from the Maoris. When we left home to go to the temple dedication, our youngest daughter, Jane, was just five years old. I promised her I would bring her some shells from New Zealand. I saw shells in people's homes, I saw them in window displays, I saw them used as decorations on restaurant tables, but no shells for sale. I tried everywhere. We were several miles from the ocean, so I couldn't gather my own. Frustrated, I told the temple matron that I thought these Maori people had really missed an opportunity. They could have gathered shells and made them available to sell to all these temple visitors and made a good piece of money.

This good sister had lived among the Maoris for some years, and she said, "Sister Hinckley, you don't understand. The beach to them is a place where you bury your feet in the warm sand, and fish, and ride the waves. It isn't a place to exploit." She said, "If you want some shells, don't try to buy any, just go into any Maori home and admire the shells you see there, and they will give them to you." I came home without any, but a little wiser.

Not only did we go to two stake conferences while in New Zealand but Brother Hinckley dedicated a library at the Church college and something like nine or ten chapels. Some were in the big cities; others were back in the mountains. The mayors of the cities turned out and occupied places on the stand. Sometimes members of Parliament were present and said very kind things about the Church. But dignitaries or no dignitaries, there were always the Maori choirs, dressed in white with flower corsages, looking beautiful and singing like angels.

We met so many of that wonderfully dedicated group of people, the labor missionaries. Those beautiful buildings in New Zealand would have been impossible without their work and your tithing. Most of the foremen and supervisors are from the United States. They have left their loved ones at home, or taken small children with them, and have subjected themselves to every kind of change you can imagine, going from place to place wherever a chapel is being built until the time comes for release. Financially, I can't imagine that they are doing any better than holding their own, but they are having a rich and rewarding experience.

I was interested in a brother from California who was supervisor for all the buildings throughout New Zealand. He traveled from dedication to dedication. Most of them were the fruits of his labors, either directly or indirectly. He made fine speeches at all the dedicatory services. And it was he who had said just six years ago when the missionaries knocked on his door in California, "Well, yes, I'll join your church, but I'm not going to do anything in it." All kinds of things—you could call them miracles—happen to all kinds of people when they lose themselves in the work of the Lord.

Next we attended stake conferences in Australia in the beautiful cities of Sydney and Brisbane. Over a thousand people. Just like Salt Lake City. Unbelievable. Australia is a vast and surprising country: beautiful, semitropical living along the coasts, vast desert covering most of the interior. We flew for hours over a section of Australian desert without seeing a sign of life.

From there we went to Vietnam (and this is beginning to sound like a travelogue), where we met with our servicepeople and the only native members in the entire country of Vietnam. Saigon, the capital of Vietnam, is a beautiful city resembling Paris, France. In fact, it is known as the Paris of the Orient. Two and one-half million people live in Saigon. The two native members are young women twenty-one and twenty-three years of age. One of them was at the airport to meet us at midnight when we arrived. I had been strapped into the jet for twelve and a half hours. I felt like an unmade bed. She was dressed in white satin trousers over which she wore a long silk apricot-colored tunic. Her hair fell to her waist, jet black and shiny clean. Her creamy olive complexion was flawless. I thought I had never seen such a vision of loveliness.

We held a meeting with the servicemen and their families and the two Vietnamese girls. I would like to read you a little from the testimony of one of these girls. I wrote down what I could remember of it.

"One thing is great surprise. My family is hardly ever sick since coming into the Church. Maybe this is one of the blessings that the Lord has given me. My family has always been so much sick and now I pray, 'Father, give my family good health.' And they are sick no more. I always try to be righteous and fair, but now I have faith. I do. I pray I may live good, like all of you, so others may be missionary girl this way.

"I have great hope as my father got some Mormon literature in French, so he could read about it. I feel my father like this religion. I want my whole family to have it. I do not know enough to teach them, but I have feeling in me that what I am learning is true. I appreciate the love you all have for me and the love I have for you."

When I was a child, I used to go to the Tabernacle at conference time with my mother and father. It was crowded, even in those days, and I can still feel the discomfort of being packed into a seat until there was no room at all for squirming. On more than one occasion, I heard President Heber J. Grant bear his testimony. He always said it in pretty much the same language, and I came to look forward to it. If he changed a word, I was disappointed. It went something like this—in a big booming voice: "I've borne my testimony from Canada on the north to Mexico on the south, in all the countries of Europe and on the islands of the sea."

How this used to thrill me and make goose bumps appear on my arms! Since then I've heard many and many a testimony, and I suspect that our testimonies are made up in a small part of testimonies of others which we have heard and to which we have responded. The testimonies I have heard have been to me the voices of angels singing. They have confirmed my belief in the Lord, just as the angels singing at the dedication of the Manti Temple confirmed my grandmother's belief in the Lord.

May we be ever grateful for the abundant miracles available to us in The Church of Jesus Christ of Latter-day Saints.

THE SAVIOR

CHRISTMAS IS A wonderful time of the year. As the season begins, we are still basking in the glow of Thanksgiving Day, when we paused to thank our Heavenly Father in a special way for our multitudinous blessings and in many instances enjoyed the company of beloved family members and friends.

And then we come into the beautiful Christmas season.

I love everything about it. I know it has become too commercial. We would all agree. But perhaps in our particular culture, that is the way we have of showing that this is the most important day of the year. I love the street lights, the Temple Square lights, the store decorations, the folks from the Salvation Army ringing their bells. Yes, even the crowds of Christmas shoppers, knowing that most of them are looking for something that might make someone happy. There is much of hustle and bustle, of gift wrapping, card sending, baking, housecleaning, phoning, and feeling concern about proper gifts for this one and that one. But the wonderful thing is that through it all there is an escalating awareness of the Savior. We will, sure as anything, read again about His birth in Luke. We will sing and listen to all kinds of music about Him, from "Away in a Manger" to *The Messiah*. But what does it all mean if it doesn't do something to us inside? The words that always jump out at me are "Come, follow me." What did Jesus do that we could follow him in doing?

Jesus went about doing good.

He healed the leper, cast out devils, raised the dead. None of this can we do in just the same way. But in the environment we find ourselves in, there is so much we can do. There is no such thing as a small act of kindness. Acts of kindness come easily at Christmas. Our grandchildren are having a great time shopping for a family who cannot provide a Christmas for their children. But there are myriads of kindnesses we can do all through the year if we are alert to them.

I would just like to share some stories about the Savior that I particularly love, things I have learned from His life concerning the invitation He repeatedly gave to us to "come, follow me."

I have loved Him since I was a child. In the bedroom where my sisters slept, Mother hung a large picture of the boy Jesus teaching the wise men in the temple. She had positioned the picture so that the first thing our eyes saw when we awakened each morning was the beautiful face of Jesus. I was grown and long gone from the home before I realized what a profound effect this had had on my life.

When the picture came into my possession in later years, I could not throw it away, although it was old and damaged. It represented my first strong feelings of love for the Savior—the beginnings of my testimony. And because it depicted the boy Jesus teaching the wise men in the temple, that story has always been one of my favorites. When I was young, I admired His adventure and His boldness in leaving His parents to talk with adult men in the temple. When I became a mother of boys myself, I was intrigued and inspired by the mother of Jesus through this experience. After I had experienced losing a child for an hour or two in a crowded place, I could now empathize with her anxiety. But how beautifully she handled it when they found Him. In her words of gentle yet unmistakable reproof, she said: "Son, why hast thou thus dealt with us? behold, thy father and I have sought thee sorrowing."

The boy's reply astonished them, in that it revealed—to an extent they had perhaps not before realized—His rapidly maturing powers of judgment and understanding. Said He, "How is it that ye sought me? wist ye not that I must be about my Father's business?" (Luke 2:49). His reply, in the words of James E. Talmage, was to Mary a reminder of what she seems to have forgotten at the moment, the matter of her son's paternity. Nevertheless, He obeyed His parents and returned with them to Nazareth. "And [Jesus] went down with them, and came to Nazareth, and was subject unto them: but his mother kept all these sayings in her heart" (Luke 2:51).

I had always wanted to go to Nazareth, and on our first trip to the Holy Land I eagerly looked forward to seeing where the boy Jesus lived. But when we arrived, we found that because of a strike we could not go to Nazareth. Then the opportunity and blessing of going to the Holy Land came again. Once again I hoped we could go to Nazareth. This time it was possible.

I will never forget that experience. We arrived in Nazareth at noon. The main street was narrow and steep, crowded with merchants selling their wares—everything from fish to nylons. The noise was deafening. Schoolchildren were on their way home for lunch. At the bottom of the street was a very large camel, and a group of children chattering with excitement gathered around it. Two boys about nine years of age were making their way up the street, one walking backwards, as they threw a ball back and forth. "Was this the way it was when Jesus was a boy?" I asked myself. "Did He go home for lunch and stop to look at a camel and throw a ball with His friends?" I began to understand more fully that even though He was divine, the Son of God, the Prince of Peace, the King of Glory, He was also mortal. He lived on the same earth we live on. He had to overcome the challenges of mortality even as you and I do. He had to discipline Himself to get up in the morning and do His chores. He had to study and learn. My love for Him knows no bounds.

Somehow He became more personal to me. I began to think of Him more when I faced the everyday challenges, knowing that He knew my feelings and would know exactly how to comfort me. "And he will take upon him their infirmities, that his bowels may be filled with mercy, according to the flesh, that he may know according to the flesh how to succor his people according to their infirmities" (Alma 7:12).

Succor according to our infirmities. To me this is summed up in the word *comfort*.

In my scripture reading lately I have become aware of the repeated mention of the word *comfort*. What a beautiful, soft, and gentle word is *comfort*.

Whether it is "to console, to soothe, to relieve, to encourage, to give strength and hope," how we need to be comforted. We all need it.

We read the papers and listen to the news. We find little comfort there. How grateful we are for the words in the scriptures:

"Therefore, let your hearts be *comforted* . . . ; for all flesh is in mine hands; be still and know that I am God" (D&C 101:16; italics added).

The Savior Himself spoke these soothing words: "Blessed are they that mourn: for they shall be *comforted*" (Matthew 5:4; italics added).

As a resurrected and glorified being, giving His last instructions to His disciples, He spoke words of reassurance: "I will not leave you comfortless: I will come to you" (John 14:18).

And then as we take that sentence and continue with His invitation from the scriptures: "Come, follow me," we understand more completely. What better way to follow Him than to comfort another?

Sometimes it takes so little. Boy skins his knee, mother kisses it. Boy grows up and leaves home. Boy is twenty-five and in the military. His tank division is put on red alert. Father and mother go to him. Father gives him a blessing. Mother hugs him. He is comforted.

How grateful we are for the privilege of praying in the name of the Savior—in the name of the boy who played in the streets of Nazareth and understands this mortal life completely, in the name of the one who sacrificed Himself that we might live again with Him and the Father, who are the ultimate sources of comfort and peace.

I know that my Redeemer lives—what comfort this sweet sentence gives! Alma, speaking to the soon-to-be baptized members of the Church by the waters of Mormon, told them they should be "willing to mourn with those that mourn; yea, and comfort those that stand in need of comfort (see Mosiah 18:9). May our willingness find words and deeds to help our brothers and sisters, now and always.

"Bless Our Missionaries in the Field and Lead Them to the Honest in Heart"

When we were in London for the dedication of the London Temple, I had my first experience of seeing our missionaries in action. This was an exciting adventure for me. For something like fifteen years my husband had worked with the missionary program. We had talked missionary talk, breakfast, lunch, and dinner. Our phone rang thousands of times with the problems of the twenty to thirty thousand missionaries who came and went during that time. So it was wonderful for me to look out of my window that beautiful morning when we arrived in London and see just a few rods away some boys in dark suits talking with little groups of people on the London Temple grounds. I flew down two flights of stairs and across a broad lawn and stood on the outside of the circle and listened. I'll never forget that experience. It overwhelmed me to see these youngsters being so bold. I thought of my young son who was still in high school, of what it took to get his eyes off the ground to meet the eyes of another. And I wondered what miracle had been wrought in these boys.

When I arrived on the scene, a young boy was speaking to the group. And I mean *boy*. He wasn't a man. He didn't appear to be old enough to drive a car, though I am sure he was. This boy was answering some questions that the open-house guests had concerning the temple, through which they had just toured. The spectators were a fine-looking, well-dressed group. Among them I noticed a woman of about thirty-six years of age who was looking at the missionary intently, never taking her eyes off him. He brought the little discussion to a close by explaining that he knew that when he said his prayers at night, he was addressing a personal being, a Father in Heaven who lived. Such boldness from a youngster! Then he asked if there were any more questions.

The woman who had never taken her eyes off him said, "Yes, I have a question. How can you be so sure of what you are saying?" And then I heard one of the most powerful testimonies I have ever heard. He said, as nearly as I can remember, "Everything in the scriptures tells me that God is a personal being, beginning in the second chapter of Genesis, which says 'And God made man in his own image and in his likeness.' And I have a testimony in my heart that He lives and is my Father in every sense of the word." The woman stood in silence, her eyes still fastened on him. What can you say in the face of such a testimony? The only thing she said was, "It's incredible!" as she made her way slowly down the path.

I overheard a young and pretty wife say to her husband as they were leaving the grounds, "My, but those young missionaries certainly do misquote the Bible, don't they, dear?" He answered, "That's the strange part about it. They didn't misquote a word." She was silent for a moment, and then said almost hesitantly, "Then, if that is so, they surely have the answers to a lot of things, don't they?" I wanted to turn and say to her, "Yes, they do have the answers, the answers to everything. They have the gospel of Jesus Christ in its fullness, if you could just humble yourselves to accept it."

I thought of the Savior's words: "O Jerusalem, Jerusalem, . . . how often would I have gathered thy children together, even as a hen gathereth her chickens under her wings, and ye would not!" (Matthew 23:37).

Those sweet, intelligent, inspired missionaries wanted to gather the British people who came to the temple grounds. When the guests left, they were given some literature together with a little slip of paper explaining that if they would like more information about the Mormons, they could fill out the slip and mail it to the mission office in London, fifty miles away. The mission president told us that they had received as many as fifty requests in one day's mail. It was heartwarming.

Missionaries do the Lord's work. They make a difference.

I hope none of you young men will cheat yourselves of the most tremendous experience that can ever come into your lives. You are going to live a good many years. Make up your mind while you are young that you are going to give two of these years to the Lord. This will be no sacrifice on your part. It is nothing short of an obligation that you have inherited. You have what you have today because back along the line somewhere, sometime, someone taught the gospel to you or one of your ancestors. The very least you can do is to do the same for someone else.

I heard a boy—his first year at the university—make the remark once that he didn't want to go on a mission because he thought every returned missionary he had ever met was kind of a sissy guy. I've never felt so much like taking issue with anyone over anything. That boy today, three years later, is married and working at a little two-cent job in California. His two younger brothers are at present in the mission field, going through the kind of rough-and-tumble experiences that this boy will never know if he could have stood up under.

Let me tell you that missionary work is not for the weak. If there is any situation in the world that will separate the men from the boys, it is missionary work. I've seen a boy shake with sobs of discouragement over problems beyond his capacity. And then I've seen him six months later, when through faith and prayer and sweat and toil he has come out the conqueror.

When you young men leave the airport for your mission field, you'll probably be nineteen years of age. Your mother and father, in spite of the love they have for you, will have spoiled you almost beyond saving. It isn't your fault. You can't help it that you have been raised in a land of luxury, where you've had a bicycle ever since you can remember and a car at your disposal since you've been old enough to care. It isn't exactly your fault that you've had three square meals a day, and plenty of snacking in between. It isn't really your fault that you've had a good bed to sleep in every single night of your life and that you have never had to go without shoes when you've needed them. This isn't really your fault.

But the result is that when you leave for your mission, you'll be a spoiled, pampered, and protected kid. Four to twelve hours later, when you arrive in the mission field, your mission president is there to welcome you, and he sees you for what you must now become. You must now become a mature man, one who knows how to work until he is weary, and who knows how to roll with the punches, and who knows when to speak and when not to speak, and who knows how to conduct himself as a representative of Jesus Christ, and who knows how to keep a press in his pants during the rainy season and his shoes shined in spite of the mud, and whose table manners are above reproach, and who knows how to put himself in the other man's shoes, and who can learn to communicate in a foreign language in six months, and who knows how to forget himself completely in the service of others. And miracle of miracles—and remember that miracles come from our Father in Heaven—most of you nineteen-year-old boys make the miraculous transition and become mature men.

One homesick boy from Idaho, the darling of his mother's eyes, the pride of his grandmother and aunts, found himself a missionary on the island of Fiji. He had a great deal of musical ability and training. He was assigned to a place where there was not even a piano, and where none cared whether he could carry a tune or not, and where the cockroaches were giving him a bad time in the cold shower. We took him out for an American hamburger to pick up his lagging spirits. It was hard to leave him. But I have confidence that he'll grow up, and he'll learn about hard knocks, and then pretty soon, he'll forget all about himself. He'll be so taken up with trying to teach someone about the gospel and so happy when he leads someone into the waters of baptism that he'll be saying, "Cockroaches? What are they?" This can happen. I know it can.

One more missionary story. On our first trip to London, we drove up to the manufacturing town of Preston, where my husband had first labored as a missionary twenty-five years before. You know how nostalgic a returned missionary is over that first field of labor! So up we went to take some pictures and reminisce.

We arrived in Preston at five o'clock in the evening. Now, this was not the beautiful, green, picturesque part of England, but the industrial area. Even so, there was a kind of stark beauty in the cobblestone streets and the long rows of chimney pots. The factories had just closed for the day, and it seemed like all of England had jammed onto the buses or were walking four abreast on the streets. They looked tired. As I looked into their faces, I felt sorry for them—sorry that they had nothing more to live for than to go to work and come home at night, with nothing more important in their lives than a cup of tea at ten and two and a pub to sit in during the evening. If only the light of the gospel could have touched them! And the most discouraging thing of all was the fact that there hadn't been a baptism in that town for over a year.

We had two elders stationed in this town, and we started out, address in hand, to find them. As we approached the flat where they had lodgings, I became apprehensive. I said to my husband, "You know, maybe we shouldn't call on these two elders. They are not expecting us, and perhaps we might find them in some situation that might embarrass them. I believe if I were a missionary in this town I might just go to bed and pull the covers over my head, or knock off for a game of tennis, or drown my discouragement in the picture show." My husband had no such misgivings, and we rang a doorbell. An English woman opened the door of a shabby but tidy flat. The smell of boiling cabbage greeted us. "Do Elders So-and-so live here?" we asked. "Come in," she said. We stepped into a narrow hall and she called up a flight of stairs, "Gary, two people here to see you." I held my breath, and in a moment two boys appeared at the top of the stairs. What a vision they were: white shirts, pressed trousers, shined shoes, looking for all the world like two handsome princes. It was all I could do to restrain myself from embracing them. Were they on the job? They were so much on the job that they hardly had time to visit with us. My husband said, "We would like to take you to dinner."

They were out the door before the sentence was finished. "No cabbage tonight!" remarked one. The senior companion hastened to explain that they were delighted to go to dinner with us, but they had three cottage meetings scheduled, the first one at six-thirty. We listened to them as we ate. Their devotion, their sincere and energetic efforts to teach the gospel to someone—anyone—in Preston were a revelation to me.

"But aren't you discouraged?" I asked.

"Discouraged about what?" they replied.

"You haven't had a baptism here in over a year!"

"Well, that doesn't mean there isn't anyone in Preston who wants the truth. And if there is someone here who is looking for the truth, we will find them."

I wouldn't have believed it without seeing it. The last we saw of those boys was the next morning as we were about to leave. In parting, they said, "Well, if we cannot be of any further help to you, we must get about our business. We are tracting a suburb on the outskirts of town and we must hurry on."

I looked at them as they marched up the street with their long, youthful strides. I said in my heart a prayer that I have repeated since I was a child, "Bless our missionaries in the field and lead them to the doors of the honest in heart."

Unsolicited, Unwelcome, and Unwanted Advice from a Seventy-Five-Year-Old Woman to College Students

THE TITLE OF my remarks is: "Unsolicited, Unwelcome, Unwanted Advice from a Seventy-Five-Year-Old Woman." There are quite a few not-so-wonderful things about growing old, so there ought to be some rewards. One of them certainly is that you can give unsolicited, unwelcome, and unwanted advice. There are other advantages, too. By the time you've reached the age of seventy-five, you are what you are. You don't have to prove anything anymore. And you are more or less accepted by others with a degree of tolerance because you are old and a little senile, of course. Our weaknesses, more often than not, are blamed on our advanced age. One woman who is the same age as President Ronald Reagan, seventy-five, said, "If President Reagan is anything like me, he must go into the Oval Office on occasion and say, 'Now, what did I come in here for?'"

I will now proceed with the unwanted advice by saying that if I were a student on a university campus, I would jump in with both feet. I would not want to be like the man who said, "I missed out on my college days. You see, I didn't enter into it quite all the way. I was afraid, I guess. I wanted to try out for a part in the school play once, but I didn't. I intended to; I went up to the room where they were reading the parts that night, but I didn't go in. There were so many there who could do it better than I, and I turned away down the hall. I wanted to try out for the football team, too, but I told myself I was too light and I turned away from the practice field. And it's funny, but you know, I can't watch a college football game, I can't listen to one on the radio, I can't watch one on television, I can't go to a college play because I see myself out on that field or on the stage where I might have been if I hadn't been afraid. And I find myself wishing that I could go back to college and live those days over again."

All about us we see dissatisfaction. We see people who want to be somebody else, or want to have someone else's talents. I suppose we're all guilty of this a little.

In the book *Woman to Woman* (Salt Lake City: Deseret Book, 1986), Norma Ashton tells a story about President Spencer W. Kimball. Spencer Kimball and Harold B. Lee were very, very dear friends. They went into the Quorum of the Twelve within a few weeks of each other. In fact, President Kimball said that he always envied his friend. He loved him so much and admired him so much he wanted to be like him in every way. And he often said, "Harold, I wish I could play the organ like you do," or "Harold, I wish I could speak like you do," or "Harold, you can see the gist of a problem so quickly. I wish my mind were as clear as yours."

Then one day, when they came out of their Thursday temple meeting, President Kimball said to President Lee, "You did a magnificent job with your report today. Oh, I wish I could do as well as you." And then he said with a twinkle in his eye, "I guess Brother Lee had had enough. He put his hands on his hips, he looked me straight in the eye. He said, 'Spencer, the Lord doesn't want you to be a Harold B. Lee. He only wants you to be the best Spencer W. Kimball you can be.'" And then he said with a smile, "After that I just tried to be the best Spencer W. Kimball I could be."

And would you say he succeeded in this?

The scripture in the Doctrine and Covenants is a comfort to me, I think it's a comfort to all of us: "For all have not every gift given unto them; for there are many gifts, and to every man [and woman] is given a gift by the Spirit of God. To some is given one, and to some is given another, that all may be profited thereby" (D&C 46:11–12). From a column by Sydney Harris in the *Deseret News* a while ago I copied the following: "Nobody knows how smart or how talented he is until he finds the incentive to use himself to the fullest." This reminds me of a young man who said to his friend, "Can you play the piano?" and the friend replied, "I don't know, I've never tried." Sydney Harris continues, "God has given us more than we know what to do with, so get going. Find out what you like to do, what you're good at, and jump in with both feet." And so I am telling you, try out for the school play or the basketball team, or dance, or track, or whatever. Even a failure can be counted as a success because it will give you experience.

Now may I quote from the *Wall Street Journal*: "The greatest waste of our natural resources is the number of people who never reach their potential. So get out of that slow lane; shift into the fast lane. If you think you can't, you won't. If you think you can, there's a good chance that you will. And even making the effort will make you feel like a new person. Don't be afraid to fail; you've failed many times, though you may not remember. You fell down the first time you tried to walk. You almost drowned the first time you tried to swim. Don't worry about failure—worry about the chances you miss when you don't even try."

And now to the second bit of unasked-for advice. If I were a student in college, I would make developing friendships on campus a very important goal. You wouldn't want to be like the man who said, "I missed out on my college days, you see, I didn't enter into it all the way. Working my way through school took all my time, or at least I said it did. Sometimes at night my roommates would gather and go for an ice cream or something. And they'd invite me to go with them. I never did. I told them I had to study. It seemed to me a lot of foolishness the way they'd go to the drive-in or loiter on the library steps, or go to snake dances and rallies. I even missed the football games. Froth, I called it, wasted time. I was in school to study. Every time I see two school chums now slap each other on the back and say, 'Remember the time . . . ,' I gulp a little because I missed out on all of that. And I find myself wishing I could go back to school and live those days over again."

Now, I'm not suggesting that you play when you should be studying, but developing friendships is important. It's a skill you will need all of your lives. No man is an island, and associating with and learning to enjoy the company of good people is a valuable part of your education.

As I pulled into a parking lot a couple of weeks ago, a car drove in beside me. It was a dear school friend of fifty-five years. We have kept in touch all through the years. I hadn't seen her for maybe three months, but our conversation picked up exactly where it left off at our last encounter. I felt so warm and comfortable in her presence, because here was a woman who knew me when I was young, and thin, and full of dreams. She understood me; she knows where I came from. Her absolute integrity and loyalty have been an inspiration to me all through the years. Her love and caring has sustained me and given me comfort when I needed it. Perhaps she has been more important to me than all the secular training that I received when I was in school.

And among the friends I would make on this campus, if I were you, is at least one of these wonderful faculty people. Each of your professors has a lot to give you that isn't in the textbooks. You might even take an apple to him. Talk to him, let him know of your desire to succeed in his class, let his or her good influence be felt in your life in a very personal way.

And now the third bit of advice. This is about becoming acquainted with those sometimes intimidating textbooks. When you open that textbook, say to yourself, "I want to know what this book has to teach me."

I found myself one day in the home of one of our wonderful Church leaders in Buenos Aires, Argentina. There were several women there. We were waiting for our husbands, as usual, who were in a meeting at the stake house. These were delightful, beautiful women whose native language, of course, was Spanish. I wanted so much to be part of that group. I was straining to catch any Spanish word I could catch, and failing miserably. Suddenly, like an old-time vision passing across my eyes, was a Spanish class that I had taken at East High School in 1928. I took the class for two years, and I could see it as plain as if I were back there. I could almost smell the chalk dust and hear that scratchy record playing "Cielito Lindo." I could see Miss Farrell, the teacher, leaning on the windowsill trying to fight back the tears because those three big bullies on the back row were completely out of control. And then I thought of Eleanor, who always sat right beside me and was always looking on my paper and popping her gum in my ear.

I did the very minimum required to get a respectable grade in that class, and I promptly put every Spanish word out of my mind when I left it. I took the class because I needed the credit. I certainly did not take it to learn Spanish. Who needed to know Spanish, anyway? I didn't know a single person who spoke Spanish. Even the teacher spoke only a few laborious sentences occasionally. And now, when Brother Hinckley and I travel through the stakes and the missions of the Church, we find that Spanish has become the second language of the Church. And we find ourselves constantly struggling to communicate with these wonderful, Spanish-speaking members whom we love so much.

I missed out. I missed out on a valuable experience because I did not have a love affair with my Spanish textbook when the opportunity was there and the time and season were right. So, no matter the class, or how irrelevant it may seem, learn, learn, learn, as if your life depended on it. Perhaps it will. Learn the thrill of digging for fossils on the mountainside, or working over a test tube until dark, or getting on the trail of something in the library and searching it down feverishly for hours. Learn to be a real student, an excellent student.

A friend of mine lost her parents when she was very young. She was raised by her grandmother, who for some reason or other never bothered to tell her anything much about her mother. One day, when my friend was in her teens, she was going through some papers in her grandmother's house, and she ran across a report card of her mother's from grade school. At the bottom of the card in a space labeled "Remarks" the teacher had written: "Excellent in every way."

This young woman clasped the card to her chest and waltzed around the room saying, "My mother was excellent. My mother was excellent in every way!" It's all she ever knew about her mother, but it inspired her the rest of her life. It *does* matter, my dear young friends, that you are excellent in every way. It matters.

And now, the fourth and, you will be glad to know, the last bit of unasked-for advice. If I were a college student, I would make religion an important part of my college life. You can't be a whole person without religion. You can't feed your body and your mind and starve your spirit. Listen one more time to the man who said: "I missed out on my college days. You see, I didn't enter into it quite all the way. I went there as a freshman and I became somewhat irritated over having to take courses in religion in order to graduate. I must be honest and say that I even cheated on some of the examinations in those courses. It was only later that I discovered that I never understood the meaning of the great principles that were being discussed. I never really understood them or internalized them. It was only after I was out of college, and the scales fell from my eyes, that I discovered that those principles, if understood and accepted and lived, would bring me the greatest joy I could ever know. It was only then, in the later years of my life, that I made the personal commitment to try to live those principles and to represent Him in the finest way that I could. I dropped into the university on another day and attended a devotional in which a great man talked about those principles, and I found myself wishing that I could go back to college and live those days over again."

Now, there are some specific ways to avoid such a disaster. One way is to make a real effort to get your very own personal testimony of the gospel of Jesus Christ. President Harold B. Lee once told us that it is vital for us to have our own testimony and not to have to lean on the testimony of others if we are to survive in the years ahead of us. And there are ways to do this. First there must be a desire to know. There must be the wanting.

If you will pardon a personal example, I would like to tell you about my testimony. Being born under the covenant, I grew up in a family of faith. My parents were totally committed to the gospel. Our lives centered on the Church. I believed because it had never occurred to me not to believe. When I was seventeen, I received my first real Church calling. It was to teach a class of boys and girls in the junior Sunday School. I was thrilled and excited. I got the manual Saturday night and began to prepare the lesson.

It now occurred to me that I was about to teach some innocent children something of which I had no personal testimony. I had only been walking on a path of belief. This upset me. I felt uncomfortable about it. I went to my father and told him of my dilemma, and, wise father that he always was, he said, "Well, why don't you read Joseph Smith's story of the First Vision, and see how you feel about it."

I went into the bedroom and closed the door, and I began to read the story that I knew almost by heart. But this time—this time—it was different. It was different because I read wanting to know, wanting desperately to know, and I wanted to know soon—before Sunday morning. By the time I had finished reading, there had come into my heart the sweet assurance that when Joseph Smith told what happened to him in the grove, he told the truth. I have never doubted it since, and I was ready and anxious to teach the children the next morning.

A story of a girl in Australia also illustrates this desire for a testimony. She graduated from high school and went to work in an ice-cream store. Her parents were very domineering and had made her feel that she wasn't worth much. So every day she dished up ice cream, and every night she went home and watched television. She was vegetating.

Then two Mormon missionaries knocked at her door. They were invited in. They began to talk. The parents were not the least bit interested in anything they said. But something they said electrified this girl. They said that she was a child of God. She said the fact that she could, in any way, have any kind of a connection with any kind of a God so shocked and intrigued her that she asked the elders if they could come back the next night and tell her more. They said no, they had another appointment. So she asked if they could come in the morning, at seven o'clock.

They went back at seven the next morning and taught her more. She went down to the ice-cream store early. She went into the back room and kneeled down to offer the first prayer of her life. She didn't know how to pray, so she simply said, "Is what these missionaries are telling me true? Am I your child?"

At that moment, she said, a beautiful feeling seemed to enter the soles of her feet and go right up through her and out the top of her head. It just enveloped her. She stood up. She said, "Thank you very much. That's all I wanted to know."

Of course she joined the Church, and as she participated in the programs, this girl blossomed like a rose. Her testimony came in response to a passionate desire to know. Desire is the very first step in gaining a testimony.

Now, perhaps we cannot all expect such an immediate and specific answer, but the desire must be there. President David O.

McKay gave a talk at priesthood meeting in general conference that may have been a bit shocking to many, since many of us are conditioned to expect that prophets have no difficulty in getting divine manifestations. President McKay told how he had struggled in vain through his teenage years to get God "to declare to me the truth of His revelations to Joseph Smith."

He prayed fervently and earnestly in the hills and at home, but had to admit to himself that "no spiritual manifestation has come to me." But he continued to seek the truth and to be active in the Church. He went on a mission largely because he trusted his parents. "Finally," President McKay said, on his mission, "the spiritual manifestation for which I had prayed as a boy in my teens came as a natural sequence to the performance of duty." That's very impressive to me. It came as a natural sequence to the performance of duty. Just as the Lord declared in John 7:17: "If any man will do his will, he shall know of the doctrine."

Now, what does this tell us about attending church, and about being actively engaged in it? You belong to a student ward here, and we know there are not enough callings to go around. But I hope you have talked to your bishop and told him that it is your desire to help in whatsoever way you can. Discipline yourselves. Get out of bed on Sunday and go to your meetings. It's important—terribly important.

I met a friend one day not long ago, a doctor at the LDS Hospital whom I hadn't seen for a little while, and I asked him casually what he was doing in the Church these days. He lit up like a Christmas tree. He said, "I have the most wonderful job I have ever had in the Church. I am a bishop of a student ward on the University of Utah campus." And then he said with tears in his eyes, and with his voice choking with emotion, "This morning, Monday morning, my twenty-year-old Relief Society president called me and said, 'Bishop, what can I do to help you this week?'" Think of that for a moment: What can I do to help you? That's what it's all about.

Some of you may say, and especially you returned missionaries, "Well, I don't need to be bothered with all that. I have a testimony. I feel secure in it. I'm okay." But let me remind you of the words of President Harold B. Lee: "Testimony isn't something you have today, and you will have always. A testimony is fragile. It is as hard to hold as a moonbeam. It is something you have to recapture every day of your life."

Brother Hinckley and I had the marvelous experience of traveling all over Europe with the Lees right after President Lee became the president of the Church. He held meetings with hundreds and hundreds of missionaries. And every time President Lee addressed a group of missionaries, every single time, he said, "Elders and sisters, your testimony has to be renewed every day." And I believe it. Sometimes it is renewed just because of a little experience, or maybe reading a verse of scripture that touches a tender spot, or turning a corner and coming upon a field of wildflowers, or seeing a newborn babe, perfect in every way. But it mostly comes from living the gospel and serving in the Church. It isn't so hard to renew your testimony daily if you are active in the Church. As President McKay said, "It comes as a natural sequence to the performance of duty."

Well, I've given you a lot of advice—and even if my advice was unsolicited, unwelcome, unwanted, and will be politely ignored, I feel so much better for having said it! In closing, though, I think you deserve to hear some advice from someone more qualified to give it than I. This is advice from one of my favorite, favorite people. It is advice from Alma the Younger. I love that man. I love him for what he has taught me, and for the way he makes me feel when I read his words. His conversion came through a very painful process. But once he was converted, he jumped in with both feet. As he grew older and was able to rid himself of the affairs of government, he began preaching the gospel, first in his hometown of Zarahemla, and then over the river in the valley of Gideon. He must have been a marvelous speaker, for the scriptures tell us that the people of Gideon responded. They followed him. They did as he asked them to do. Not one hundredth part of the things he said to the people of Gideon has been recorded, but what we do have is pertinent to us today.

These were his parting words to the people of Gideon: "I would that ye should be humble, and be submissive and gentle; easy to be entreated; full of patience and long-suffering; being temperate in all things; being diligent in keeping the commandments of God at all times; asking for whatsoever things ye stand in need, both spiritual and temporal; always returning thanks unto God for whatsoever things ye do receive. And see that ye have faith, hope, and charity, and then ye will always abound in good works" (Alma 7:23–24).

And now, my dear young friends, as the years rush on and you look back on your college days, I hope that you will say, "I lived those days to the fullest, and I am happy."

To Women: "Is This What I Was Born to Do?"

THIS IS A Cinderella story, but it has far more substance than Grimm's fairy tale.

Once upon a time, many, many years ago, lived a king who reigned over India and Ethiopia, over a hundred and seven and twenty provinces. In the third year of his reign, he made a feast to show the riches of his glorious kingdom. On the seventh day of the merriment, he sent for his queen, Vashti, to show off her beauty to the people. She refused to come. The king was angry and took from her the royal crown and estate to give to another. The search began for a new queen, and beautiful women were brought from all the provinces.

Now, in one of the provinces lived a Jew whose name was Mordecai. He had raised his uncle's daughter, Esther, since her parents had died. So it came to pass that Mordecai brought Esther to the palace. All the maidens who were brought to be presented to the king were trained and groomed for one year in the women's court at the palace. Finally, it came Esther's turn to be presented to the king. And the king loved Esther above all the women he had seen, and she obtained grace and favor in his sight, and he set the royal crown upon her head and made her his queen.

Now it came to pass that the king's chief adviser hated the Jews and persuaded the king to have all the Jews in his kingdom put to death, and the king agreed to have them all annihilated, men, women, and children, on a certain date.

Mordecai tried to encourage Esther to go to the king and plead for her people. But no one, not even the queen, could enter the presence of the king without being invited. The punishment was death. She would also have to confess that she was a Jew, which the king did not know.

Mordecai tried to encourage her to do what she and only she could do, saying: "Who knoweth whether thou art come to the kingdom for such a time as this?" (Esther 4:14).

She asked Mordecai to call upon all the Jews in the land to fast for three days and pray for her. She said, "I also and my maidens will fast likewise; and so will I go in unto the king, which is not according to the law: and if I perish, I perish" (Esther 4:16).

Of course, you all know the end of the story. I have left out many of the details. Her people were saved, and Mordecai was brought into the palace as the king's chief adviser. At this point, Grimm would end his fairy tale with, "They all lived happily ever after."

We do not know the end of this story. But we do know that whenever we think of women, we celebrate Esther's very high type of courage, loyalty, and patriotism.

My favorite line of the story is Mordecai's question to her: "Who knoweth whether thou art come to the kingdom for such a time as this?"

Now, let me change the time in history and tell you of an experience I encountered on a Church assignment. This one was in Medford, Oregon, where my husband was assigned to visit a stake conference. We drove from Salt Lake City, arriving at the stake president's home late Saturday afternoon. Some of the children were home. The mother was not. The children told us she was over at the church practicing with the roadshow cast. The twelve-year-old showed us to our bedroom. It was obviously the parents' room. Everything was shiny and clean. The bathroom opening off it had been freshly painted. The paint was barely dry. It was probably finished at midnight on Friday in anticipation of our visit! The fourteen year-old had just taken a freshly baked blueberry pie from the oven. She had picked the berries that morning and baked the pie herself. On the piano were pictures of the children. They went through them for us. "And who is this one?" I asked, pointing to one on the lamp table of a young man in a white shirt, tie, and dark suit.

"Oh, that's our missionary," she replied with pride. "He's not really our brother, but he came to live with us two years ago, when his parents divorced."

It was soon time for Mother to come home. I knew exactly what she would look like. I had seen her a thousand times in other Mormon homes across the country—a typical, happy, terribly busy mother with the whir of Mormon life going on around her.

I mention these two contrasting experiences to remind you of the very different circumstances that women find themselves in. Perhaps we might take a look at our lives—either in Medford, Oregon, or in the time of King Ahasuerus—and ask ourselves, "Is life fair? Is this what I was born to do?"

Or we might change that question, "Is this what I was born

to do?" to another: "Who knoweth whether thou art come to the kingdom for such a time as this?"

President Kimball has said: "Remember, in the world before we came here faithful women were given certain assignments while faithful men were foreordained to certain priesthood tasks. . . . You are accountable for those things which long ago were expected of you."

Therefore, it would seem important that our greatest quest is to live worthy to know what the Lord's will is regarding us— what we are meant to do.

I love the scripture in the New Testament where the angel appeared to Mary, who was to become the mother of Jesus, and gave her that particular assignment. And she said, "Be it unto me according to thy word" (Luke 1:38).

Some of us are married. Some of us are not (yet). Some of us have children and grandchildren. Some have none. Some are widowed, some divorced. But we can all do what is our responsibility to do. We can all bless lives.

I quote from Elaine Cannon: "A woman's significant role is that of being an influence wherever she is. It is her role not only to give life, but to shape life."

Some women are natural leaders. Elaine Cannon is an example to me of leadership. When she served as the Young Women General President she organized 1,000 Young Women—all with beautiful banners they had made to express their commitment to the gospel—dressed in white and marched them down the streets of Salt Lake City on the 24th of July to inspire us.

I said, "Thank you." Only an Elaine Cannon could dream up and execute such a spectacle, and we were all cheered and lifted by it. She blessed us all with her leadership. The examples of such inspiring women leaders are all around us.

Some of us are followers, and that is good also, because a leader would have no one to lead without followers. Some of us are what I call "supporters." I concluded long ago that my happiest role was that of a supporter. To me personally, this is a great and extremely satisfying role.

During World War II, we were encouraged to plant gardens, not only by the Church but by the government. My husband dug 3,000 holes in the property to the south of our home and planted 3,000 tomato plants. He hoed them and weeded them and irrigated them at 4:30 every Monday morning. When the tomatoes were ripe, I spent my days picking them. Baskets full, boxes full. We put up a sign: "Tomatoes for Sale." Toward the end of the crop, we couldn't give them away. My back ached.

I could have said, "Is this what I was born to do?"

But the tomatoes went on people's food shelves, and the money we were paid for them paid the taxes that year, the taxes on our house, the house that gave us shelter and was a home for our children. The whole project gave my husband and me a sense of "togetherness." The wife does not walk in front of or behind her husband, but at his side. And what is a blessing for him is a blessing for her. I have never felt to apologize to anyone for my supporting role as a wife and mother.

Let me tell you about a beautiful girl, who during the first year of her married life lived in New York City. She had graduated from BYU in fashion design and was blessed to find an exciting job in the corporate headquarters of J.C. Penney, near Rockefeller Center. Her very responsible job was to choose what clothes would go into a large section of their catalog, which went to catalog subscribers all across the nation. It was exciting. She loved it.

Then came the impending arrival of a first baby. One day, a few months before the baby was born, she told her boss that she would soon resign. Her co-workers couldn't believe it. Why would she give up a promising career in New York to become "just a housewife"?

"I'm not leaving to become a housewife," she said. "I'm leaving to become a homemaker, the most wonderful career of all."

JoAnn Ottley, wife of the conductor of the Mormon Tabernacle Choir and an accomplished soprano, has blessed our lives with her beautiful music. She has successfully combined a partial career with homemaking. I heard her husband say that when she had finished her studies in Europe and the opportunities were there for her to become a professional opera star, she said to her husband, "I would rather go home and sing to my Relief Society sisters."

She did just that, but as the years have passed she has had more than enough opportunities to improve upon her talents and yet rear her family, too.

I once heard the story of a lawyer, the daughter of Supreme Court Justice Powell, who left her law profession to stay home with her firstborn. She said, "Anyone can take care of my clients. Only I can be the mother of this child." Her decision was easily made—not in terms of rights, but in terms of responsibility and love.

I would like to read to you the beautiful words of Neal Maxwell on this subject. "When the real history of mankind is fully disclosed, will it feature the echoes of gunfire or the sound of lullabies? The great armistices made by military men or the peacemaking of women in homes and neighborhoods? Will what happened in the cradles and kitchens prove to be more controlling than what happened in congress?

"When the surf of centuries has made the great pyramids so much sand, the everlasting family will still be standing, because it is a celestial institution."

Having said all this for the benefit of those who feel they are only housewives and mothers, I also want to pay tribute to the women who for a variety of reasons are combining child rearing with careers outside of the home. It isn't easy for you. You are working very hard, long hours, for you understand, also, the importance of home and child rearing. And you are in many instances unbelievably successful in both areas.

Each of us—married, single, widowed, divorced, housewives, career women, students, grandmothers—can ask ourselves each morning, "What can I do to make life happier for someone today?" Sometimes all it takes is just a few kind words to a clerk in the grocery store. Sometimes it is steady service over a lifetime.

Let me tell you about my grandfather's sister, who was an important person in my childhood. Aunt Nellie was a nurse. She never married. But when Mother's babies were born, she would come up from her home in American Fork and move in with us for a week or so and take care of Mother and the new baby. She has been gone now for over fifty years, but when my ninety-one-year-old mother was floating in and out of consciousness during her last illness, she kept saying, "Oh, if only Nellie were here. She could make me comfortable."

We all have our place, our important something we can do in

our own individual way—something no one else can do for us—our own unique opportunity to serve.

And let us approach our duties with an attitude of excellence. As Anne Osborn Poelman wrote: "One only has to look at a sunset, or a starry night, to know that God did everything in excellence, not in a cheap or easy way."

I read in the paper of a woman who had made an excellent career as a cleaning woman. She had gone to work after the death of her husband. She was untrained, and the most immediate work she could find was to become a cleaning woman. She became so proficient and innovative in finding the very best and most efficient and inexpensive ways to perform all the household cleaning jobs that she ended up writing and publishing a book on the subject.

The gospel calls to us to stretch ourselves, to embrace our talents, to concentrate on our strengths, to be productive, to be creative, to reach our full potential, which few of us ever do. In the words of Robert Louis Stevenson: "To be what we are and to become what we are capable of becoming is the only end of life."

Let us not waste our time saying with bitterness, "Is this what I was born to do?" Let us rather ask ourselves the question that was asked Esther: "Who knoweth whether thou art come to the kingdom for such a time as this?"

Perhaps what you are doing, whatever it is or however humble your offering, could be something that no one else could do in quite the same way. Say to yourself: "The world is my oyster. I am in control. There is no limit to what I can do."

Be thankful and be glad!

I truly believe that if we keep the commandments as we understand them and accept our responsibilities with gladness, the day will come in the eternities when God will say to us, male and female: "Well done, thou good and faithful servant: thou hast been faithful over a few things, I will make thee ruler over many things" (Matthew 25:21).

God bless us all to this end.

Building the Kingdom
from a Firm Foundation

WE ARE IN A time when the winds of adversity and sophisticated criticism and bitter attack have become the order of the day. It therefore becomes the exciting responsibility of those of us who have inherited a firm foundation from the faithful ones who preceded us to build the kingdom, while others may wear out their lives trying to destroy it.

President Spencer W. Kimball said: "We had full equality as [our Father's] spirit children. . . . Within those great assurances, however, our roles and assignments differ." (*Ensign*, November 1979, p. 102.) So your way of strengthening your faith and building the kingdom is different from my way because our roles and assignments are different. Some of us are married; some are not. Some of us have children and grandchildren and even great-grandchildren. Some have none. Some are widowed, some divorced. Some are affluent. Some live on the edge of poverty. Some are students; others have full-time careers. Some are full-time homemakers.

It is the mothers of young children I would like to address first. These are golden years for you. These are years when you will probably do the most important work of your lives. Don't wish away your years of caring for small children. Life is what happens to you while you are making other plans. This is a time of great opportunity for you to build the kingdom. When you teach children to love their Heavenly Father, you have done one of the greatest things you will ever do. If you can be a full-time homemaker, be grateful. If not, you must do what is best for you. I for one have never felt a need to apologize for my role as a full-time homemaker.

These are busy, busy days for you. I have seen women in all kinds of circumstances—Chinese women working on road repairs, European women working in the fields, Asian women sweeping streets—but it is my opinion that American women, especially Mormon women, are among the hardest working women in the world. They plant gardens and bottle the produce; they sew and bargain shop. They go on the heart fund drive. They take dinners to new mothers and the sick in their neighborhoods. They take care of aged parents. They climb Mount Timpanogos with Cub Scouts, go to Little League games, sit on the piano bench while Jennie practices, do temple work, and worry about getting their journals up-to-date. My heart bursts with pride when I see them come into church on Sunday, some as early as 8:30 in the morning, their children all clean and shiny, their arms loaded with supplies, as they head for classes where they teach other women's children. They scrub their house with little or no domestic help and then try to be the glamour girl in their husband's life when he arrives home at night. But remember, my dear young friends, that you are now doing the work that God intended you to do. Be grateful for the opportunity.

My concern for you is that you are trying to cover all the bases at one time. You cannot be everything to everyone all the time. Sister Belle S. Spafford, in her parting words to the Relief Society sisters in the Tabernacle some years ago, said:

"The average woman today, I believe, would do well to appraise her interests, evaluate the activities in which she is engaged, and then take steps to simplify her life, putting things of first importance first, placing emphasis where the rewards will be greatest and most enduring, and ridding herself of the less rewarding activities.

"The endless enticements and demands of life today require that we determine priorities in allocating our time and energies if we are to live happy, poised, productive lives." (*A Woman's Reach* [Salt Lake City: Deseret Book Co., 1974], p. 23.)

This does not mean, however, that you should have nothing in your hands but a broom and a dustpan and nothing in your head but laundry procedures and economical casseroles. Be creative. Reach out and embrace the things this wonderful world has to offer. I met a mother in Florida who was taking a class in, of all things, bird watching. It was exciting to walk through Cypress Gardens with her and share her enthusiasm for the birds that abound there. To her children a sparrow will never again be just a sparrow.

The danger and challenge is that much of what we do does not have eternal consequences. Much of the time we are running to and fro and spinning our wheels. And much of what we do is for the wrong reasons. When my neighbor had a son in grade school, the PTA was raising money by having a cookie sale once a week during the noon hour. The students paid a nickel for a cookie. Each class had a turn to furnish the cookies. It came my neighbor's turn to send a dozen cookies to school with her Ronald. The day preceding was a hectic day. No time for baking cookies. But how could she not send homemade cookies? What kind of mother would they think she was? It was after midnight when she took the cookies out of the oven. The next morning she proudly send Ronald to school with a dozen homemade, beautifully decorated cookies. When Ronald came home from school that day she asked, "Well, did you buy a cookie at noon?" "Yeah," he responded, "but by the time I got to the table all the store-bought cookies were gone. I had to buy a homemade one."

I love the scripture from Doctrine and Covenants 10:4: "Do not run faster or labor more than you have strength." Choose carefully each day that which you will do and that which you will not do, and the Lord will bless you to accomplish the important things that have eternal consequences. Let me tell you of two women who have done this under some difficult circumstances.

Ann is a single parent, a divorcée. While some divorcées feel that there is no place for them in this society, and especially in the Church environment, Ann has kept her eye on the big picture and moved steadily forward. It has not been easy, especially when her children were young. It was a challenge to provide both physically and spiritually for her two sons and one daughter, but she taught them well. Now both her sons and her daughter have filled missions. Ann went back to the University of Utah to increase her education and her earning power. While she was in school she took care of an unfortunate woman who was practically housebound. This job gave her some much needed money, while she also performed a loving service. And, believe it or not, during this time she was the Relief Society president in a large, family-oriented ward. She ran that organization as if she had nothing else in the world to do.

At the end of her next-to-last quarter in school, the grant that made it possible for her to attend school ran out. Her recently returned missionary son said, "Don't worry, Mom; we'll get you through." The dean called her in. He had gone over her record and had concluded that her work had been so outstanding that the university would waive the student teaching requirement and the rest of her class work and make her eligible for graduation with the upcoming June graduating class. The Lord blessed her because she learned early to eliminate the unnecessary and do the things that had eternal consequences. She operated from a firm foundation of faith. In so doing she blessed her children and helped to build the kingdom.

Another woman who looked toward the eternal consequences of her actions was Francie. As a child Francie suffered embarrassment when she walked out of a lighted area into the dark because she often walked into a light pole or stepped into a hole or ran into objects that she could not see because she suffered from night blindness.

She loved the outdoors and spent the summers of her early childhood in Rico, Colorado, a mining town in the beautiful Colorado Rockies. The summer after the fourth grade she was walking around the small town one evening with some friends. The girls were looking up and talking about the stars. Francie wondered why she could not see them.

By age sixteen or seventeen she found that she could not see many things at night. The doctors were puzzled, and though she felt some frustration, she compensated for her problem in various ways. One was to simply avoid going places she didn't know well at night, even some places in the house, or she would find a friend to use as a guide. Her frustrations were mounting, but perhaps it was fortunate that she did not know what was ahead of her.

At the end of high school she began to set her goals with incredible drive and faith for one so young. In three years she graduated from BYU with honors, the first young woman to graduate in youth leadership with an outdoor emphasis. She had more than once completed the BYU survival trips in the rugged desert and had proved to herself that if she capitalized on what she had and did not give in to her limitations, she could do anything.

Upon graduation she served a mission to Italy and was known as the "sergeant" because she worked so hard and encouraged others to do the same. While on her mission she found that she could no longer read the small print in the scripture footnotes. Immediately upon her return home she was diagnosed by the family ophthalmologist as having retinitis pigmentosa, an irreversible disease of the retina, which would eventually lead to total blindness.

This upsetting news did not stop her. Once again she packed her bags and left home, this time for Michigan State University in Lansing where she completed her master's degree in educational curriculum and then continued to do all the course work for her Ph.D.

While in Michigan, she met her husband, and now they have four lovely children. At this writing, she is legally blind. She is employed part-time at the University of Michigan as an academic adviser.

She pursues her church work with vigor, is a Cub Scout leader, and serves in the Primary presidency, and always she is a missionary. She has taught in the women's organizations by having a friend record the lessons from the manual on tape to which she listens and stores up the information in her mind. She works as a volunteer in the school her children attend. They go as a family to community activities, lectures, and museums. By necessity she has chosen carefully that which she will do and has concentrated on those things that have eternal consequences.

"The scriptures give me comfort and direction in the things that are most important to do," she says. "I have learned to work with what I have rather than what I don't have. I have strong feelings about my good heritage with noble ancestors who worked hard to do the things they felt were right. Their good qualities are something I can capitalize on. I have a spiritual heritage from my Heavenly Father. I have felt His divine guidance and have received blessings that are beyond measure and sometimes beyond what I deserve."

We are talking here about faith and building the kingdom from a firm foundation. May I say to Francie, "You, Francie, *are doing it* and sweeping us all onto a higher plane in the process. We are learning from you about courage and faith and building the kingdom."

And now a word to women who, for various reasons, are part-time or full-time career women. Today is your day, sisters. Never have there been so many doors open to women. It was not too long ago when, according to a report made by the University of Utah, more than half the women graduated in six majors: elementary education, English, home economics, sociology, history, and nursing.

These are very worthy pursuits. But the opportunities are widening, and more and more we see women getting law degrees, medical degrees, MBA's, degrees in computer science, and even degrees in electrical engineering. What a tremendous contribution they are making in the business world. Our women bring to the corporate world a firm but soft touch. Hardly realizing it, they bring a special quality of friendship, flexibility, love, and understanding to the professional environment. They are making this a better place for all of us, as their faith and integrity and their understanding of right and wrong flavor everything they do.

And now to my peers. On my seventieth birthday I repeated to myself all day long something I heard Stephen L Richards's wife say when she was in her nineties. She said, "Oh, to be seventy again! You can do anything when you are seventy."

Contrary to rumor, these *are* golden years, if you have a measure of good health. At this age, my dear contemporaries, we no longer have to compete with anyone. We don't have to prove anything—we just have to enjoy it all. How many of you have told your children how wonderful it is to be this age?

In 1985 Sister Camilla Kimball addressed the Women's Conference at BYU. She was ninety years old at the time and still going strong, perhaps not physically, but certainly spiritually and mentally. She inspired us all with her continuing drive to learn and her ability to make us all reach beyond our inclinations. And later, at age ninety-two, she took up oil painting.

There is so much we can do to be an influence, perhaps not in ways we have once known, but in many other ways. Last year in the Upland Terrace School in the Granite School District, which three of my grandchildren attend, grandparents gave the equivalent of two hundred hours of volunteer service. Who can measure the worth of a grandmotherly or grandfatherly influence in the classroom!

You will appreciate a letter written to Ann Landers that appeared in the newspaper some time ago. "Dear Ann Landers," it began. "I am a twenty-two-year-old graduate student who would like to express my admiration for some people who have taught me more than all the books I ever read." If you are over seventy, you can take this personally:

"Dear Older American, I want you to know how much you have improved the quality of my life. Today I was driving down the street. You were sauntering uptown, your white hair shining in the sun, a smile on your face. You waved when I went by, though you had no idea who I was.

"On my first job as a cashier, I was nervous and scared. The line was long and everyone was impatient. You let the others go first because you didn't mind waiting. When your turn came you said: 'Take your time. My, but you have pretty eyes.' I could have kissed you.

"You say, 'Have a nice day,' in the elevator and talk about the weather. I can tell by your gnarled hands that you've done a lot of hard work and I admire that.

"You have an aura of calmness that so many of my generation will never know in their mad rush for money and status. Thanks, Older American, for being there."

So if we are too tired to go mountain climbing with the grandchildren, it's all right. We can still reach out and lift someone.

Sisters, we are all in this together. We need each other. Oh, how we need each other. Those of us who are old need you who are young. And, hopefully, you who are young need some of us who are old. It is a sociological fact that women need women. We need deep and satisfying and loyal friendships with each other. These friendships are a necessary source of sustenance. We need to renew our faith every day. We need to lock arms and help build the kingdom so that it will roll forth and fill the whole earth.

A Love Unlike
Any Other Love

WHENEVER THE HYMN "We Thank Thee, O God, for a Prophet" was sung in the presence of President Spencer W. Kimball, he would join in with enthusiasm, thinking, he said, not in terms of himself as president of the Church, but of all the prophets who had gone before. So it is with Mother's Day. We hear the beautiful music and tributes paid to mothers and we think not of ourselves, but of our own mothers and other mothers who have warmed our hearts and nurtured and inspired us.

A succession of mothers who have been instrumental in shaping my life started five generations back with Sarah, the earliest on my matriarchal line to join the Church.

Sarah grew up in a home of refinement in Cambridge, England, and was well educated for a woman of her time. Her husband died at the young age of thirty-two, leaving her with three daughters and one son, and a family business. He had wanted his children reared in a church, so they affiliated with the Church of England shortly after his death. A Mr. Goates called regularly at her home with butter, eggs, and bakery products, and on occasion she would chat with him on current topics, including religion. She became so intrigued with his explanations of the Bible that she asked to what church he belonged. When he told her he belonged to The Church of Jesus Christ of Latter-day Saints, her curiosity was aroused. He brought her literature to read. This she studied diligently, searching the scriptures to verify the truths she was seeking. At first her children disapproved of their mother's association with the baker, whom they thought of inferior class. They were humiliated when she took them to the town hall to hear the Mormon missionaries. As time passed, however, her daughters became interested and decided to join the Church with their mother. Sarah was the first woman to be baptized in Cambridge. Three days after the girls were baptized, Sarah's only son died suddenly.

Soon Sarah began thinking of emigrating to Zion. Her parents were distraught and tried to dissuade her. They begged her to stay in England so the girls could continue their education at Cambridge College. They offered her three hundred pounds more from their estate if she would remain at home. She replied that she could not accept their offer, that she felt impelled to go to Zion. She sold her business and began her preparations.

On February 23, 1851, Sarah and her daughters left Cambridge. What dauntless faith and courage they possessed! They left their loved ones and friends, never to see them again. They left the comforts of a well-established home, the security of a thriving business, educational opportunities for the girls, and a gracious way of life, all to go to an unknown, strange, and undeveloped land. It was a bold step, an expression of the strength of Sarah's testimony and of her desire to live the gospel in Zion and to do what seemed best for her daughters. This faith and commitment went down into the very bones of her children and her children's children.

Sarah's daughter Charlotte was seventeen when the family

made the long journey from England. Charlotte became my great-grandmother. When they were ten days out at sea, she recorded in her diary: "The sea is calm and beautiful. The wind is in our favor and although I long to see my friends in Cambridge, I console myself in the thought that I am going to Zion, the promised land. Oh! glorious thought."

Before a year had elapsed, Charlotte was married to the young man who played the bugle on their trek across the plains. To this union were born twelve children. The first arrived when she was eighteen, in a covered wagon and with no one to attend her. This beautiful and gentle young mother faced all the rigors, disappointments, and sorrows of pioneer life. She lost two sons in death within a year, one twelve years old and the other fourteen. She did not complain when her husband was called to serve a mission in England, leaving her to provide money for him and a living for the children. She did not complain when he returned home after thirteen months because of ill health and died only a few weeks later, leaving her alone, at the age of forty-three.

Like other pioneer women, Charlotte did whatever needed to be done. She not only cared for her family, nurturing, teaching, guiding, and loving them, but was also active in charitable work. She gathered money for the construction of the Manti Temple. She gathered wheat for the Relief Society storage bins, made burial clothes, and nursed those who were sick. When the call came for the Saints to raise silkworms for the manufacture of silk in Utah, she planted twenty-four mulberry trees to feed the worms. Through all the hardships of a rugged pioneer life, she was always cheerful. What she did, she did with joy—joy in the gospel, joy in life itself, and joy in her children. Her two granddaughters, who grew up next door to her, said they never heard their grandmother raise her voice or speak a cross word. She was indeed a saintly woman, a mother to be honored.

Next came Charlotte's daughter Martha Elizabeth. She was the ninth child of this family of twelve in Nephi, Utah. When Martha was nineteen, she married George Paxman and moved to Manti, where George was working on the Manti Temple. They did not have much by way of worldly goods, but they had enough for their needs. George worked eight hours a day on the temple and received only a weekly order of four dollars at the local store. The balance of his compensation came from the Tithing Office. But it was a labor of love. He was building a temple to God. Their joy was increased with the birth of a blue-eyed baby girl near the end of their first year in Manti.

On June 27, 1887, a month before little Frances was one year old, George staggered home in great pain from work on the temple, where he had hung one of the heavy east doors. He was taken to Nephi by team and wagon and then to Provo, where he died three days later of a strangulated hernia.

Martha's world collapsed. She returned to her mother's home in Nephi, and eight months later she gave birth to another daughter, whom she named Georgetta, after her beloved George. She then moved into a small adobe house next door to her mother and struggled to begin a new life with her little girls. She became an expert seamstress. Sometimes she took them with her into the homes where she sewed for two or three days at a time. Sometimes she sewed in her own home late into the night after they were in bed. Her gifted hands turned out an incredible quantity of beautiful handwork: crocheted doilies, tablecloths, afghans, lace collars, beaded purses, and many other items. Always she kept the girls close to the Church. She taught them the things of God. She read to them from the best books. She was meticulous about paying a full tithing.

When the girls finished school in Nephi, Martha moved to Salt Lake City, rented a small home, and went to work in the alterations department of a department store. One of her daughters attended the LDS Business College and the other went to the University of Utah on a scholarship.

Martha, an attractive woman, had offers of marriage after the death of her husband, but she chose not to marry again. The principle of eternal marriage to George sustained her through sixty-six years of widowhood. She had unshakable faith in the gospel and played the sacred role of motherhood as a single parent in a magnificent way.

Martha's daughter Georgetta was my mother. I could write a book about the things my mother taught her children, but I mention only a few. She inherited from the three mothers who preceded her the spirit of sacrifice for the gospel and for her children. Her unconditional love for the Lord and for her children was ever present. Having grown up in a family where there was no priesthood, she never got over the wonder of having a husband who held and honored the priesthood of God.

One of my earliest memories is of sitting by the dining room stove with Mother when the younger children had gone to bed, waiting for Father to come home from MIA. I can still see him coming through the door with snow on his hat and coat. He and Mother then talked and laughed about what had gone on. I thought his being the MIA president must be the most wonderful thing that could happen to a family. And so it was down the years with many Church callings. It was the same when he grew older and was ordained a patriarch. When people came to our home for blessings, Mother was her happiest. She would have the house in immaculate order, with fresh flowers and an air of happiness permeating every room.

Thus she prepared me, without realizing it, to live happily with a man whose total commitment to the Lord has dictated our lifestyle. I cannot remember a time when our five children were growing up that their father was able to sit with us in church. He was always on a church assignment. Because of the home in which I grew up, it did not occur to me that there was any other way to live. Mother had taught us by example that the most wonderful thing in the world is to have a husband who loves the Lord. It wasn't that she ever openly said this; it was her ever constant attitude.

There is nothing so powerful in the world as the example of a righteous mother, and to have four generations of blessed mothers to sustain and uphold and inspire is a blessing beyond measure.

Now we have a generation of new mothers in a different kind of world, different from the pioneer lifestyle but with its own unique and sometimes overwhelming challenges. Their children are growing up in a world where Satan is making his presence felt in every facet of life. Evil in every form is swirling about them—disrespect, irresponsibility, negative criticism, offensive language, dishonesty, immorality, drugs, and the sometimes questionable advantage of too much affluence. How marvelous are the mothers who are nurturing and strengthening the youth of today. How valiant they are in making their homes a refuge from the evils that could otherwise engulf them.

In his book *Everything But Money*, author Sam Levenson tells of growing up in a crowded New York tenement where the environment was anything but genteel. But his wonderful mother was dedicated to making respectable and upright adults of her eight precocious children. He writes, "The fight against individual corruption was part of the fight against the environment. The moral standard of the home had to be higher than that of the street. 'You are not on the street; you are in our home. This is not a cellar nor a poolroom. Here we act like human beings.' I remember the speech well. Like royalty, Mama said 'we.'" (*Everything But Money* [New York: Pocket Books, 1966], p. 123.)

And so it is with the mothers of today. They are committed to loving their children into standing on higher ground than the environment surrounding them. We see young mothers coming into church on a Sunday with their children, all with clean, shiny hair, shoes polished, dresses and suits looking as if they were on their way to the photographer, and the mothers' arms filled with books and supplies as they head for classes to teach yet other children. There can be weariness and frustration in these motherly activities, but there is also joy.

And what do you do with mother love when the babies are grown and gone away? Well, another child of a new generation is born and the whole process starts over again. The caring, the loving, the nurturing. The greatest miracle of all—the assurance that life will never end. There will always be mothers, and they will always be endowed with a love that is unlike any other love on the face of the earth.

INDEX